Computer Graphics: Systems and Applications

Managing Editor: J. L. Encarnação

Editors: K. Bø   J. D. Foley   R. A. Guedj
P. J. W. ten Hagen   F. R. A. Hopgood   M. Hosaka
M. Lucas   A. G. Requicha

Springer
Berlin
Heidelberg
New York
Barcelona
Budapest
Hong Kong
London
Milan
Paris
Tokyo

Adelino Santos

Multimedia and Groupware for Editing

With 49 Figures

 Springer

Adelino Santos

Bernhardstr. 1
D-64291 Darmstadt, FRG

Cataloging-in-Publication Data applied for

Die Deutsche Bibliothek – CIP Einheitsaufnahme:
Santos, Adelino: Mulitmedia and groupware for editing / Adelino Santos. - Berlin; Heidelberg;
New York; Barcelona; Budapest; Hong Kong;
London; Milan; Paris; Tokyo: Springer, 1995 (Computer graphics)
ISBN-13:978-3-642-79867-2

ISBN-13:978-3-642-79867-2   e-ISBN-13:978-3-642-79865-8
DOI: 10.1007/978-3-642-79865-8

Cover Design: Konzept & Design, Ilvesheim
Typesetting: Camera-ready by author
SPIN: 10484599   33/3142 - 5 4 3 2 1 0 - Printed on acid-free paper

Preface

Nowadays, multimedia techniques enable the production of non-traditional documents containing enormous amounts of information. The production of this kind of documents by a group, as opposed to an individual, is the main motivation of this book. To work properly, a group needs to communicate: more than enhancing the contents of documents, multimedia technology can also be used to enhance the communication channels within a group. How these factors (multimedia documents and communication and groups of authors) fit together are the main questions to be tackled here. As an example of how these notions might be found together, we elaborated a conceptual framework for cooperative multimedia editing, built a prototype system and used it to conduct a group effectiveness study. This example can be extrapolated to other multimedia groupware. This way, this work relates the following three notions: multimedia communication, cooperative multimedia editing and group support and effectiveness.

The past forty years have seen dramatic advances in information and telecommunication technologies, and the widespread adoption of these technologies bears the best testimony to the advent of the "information society". According to a study launched by the Commission of the European Community, telecommunication will be a driving force in the Europe economy at the beginning of the next millennium with an estimated annual growth rate of 8%, as compared to e.g. the car industry with only 2%.

To succeed, cooperative multimedia editing software will have to be used by most or all group co-authors. This means appealing to people with different roles, backgrounds and preferences. In addition, group dynamics can be complex, can vary widely from setting to setting and are not completely understood. An important trade-off involved in designing editing functionalities is the level of functionality. With fewer functionalities, there is less for the co-authors to learn and fewer decisions to make. But each new capability can, once learned, make the situations it was designed for easier. If the tool takes too much time to learn, it either will not be used or will disrupt the cooperation. Altogether, any designer's or programmer's intuition will be a less reliable guide than has been true for single-user applications.

Instead, cooperation takes place because of the necessity to overcome the limited capabilities of individuals. People believe that tasks cannot be accomplished by an individual as quickly, as efficiently or as well as by a group. Typical editing sessions involve 2 to 3 participants. It is still unclear if this will remain so for computer-supported editing sessions, because people will no longer have the problem of physically accessing the editing surface (board, paper). Also, they take place wherever people get together and have conversations, not only in meeting rooms. This way, group work differs from individual work in several aspects:

- It involves extensive person-to-person communication. Consequently, any product supporting group work must have a variety of communication capabilities which can be customised for individual members;

- Because the overall task is partitioned among a number of workers, there is a task management function that must be performed. This involves assignment, status monitoring, integration of individual work and their assembly into a deliverable unit;

- There can be many different groups within organisations: committees, project teams, formal authority groups, peer groups or information exchange networks. Therefore, the relationship of the group to the larger entity, of which it is part, needs to be considered. This includes such issues as culture, structure, power, authority, norms and values;

- There are processes, beyond those necessary for individual workers, that need to be supported: roles, interaction protocols and procedures must be established and interpersonal activities must be attended to;

These properties can become disadvantageous for groups aiming at being as efficient as individuals. They appear problematic for managers and supervisors who are concerned with productivity, and create frustration for individual workers. The development of software that is designed or can be used to support the kind of activities work groups perform has to solve problems which are different from the ones involved in traditional software design. The main difference is that unlike software designed for word processing, data analysis or data visualisation, group software is intended to aid work groups, project teams or whole organisations rather than to support the completion of specific tasks by an individual.

To sum up, as a scientific field, multimedia communication, multimedia processing and CSCW are still in their infancy and theoretical problems abound. Problems and open questions touch on the three notions mentioned above and have both a general and a specific character. General questions are:

- How can diverse media enrich the information conveyed by documents?

- What media or media combination can be used in the communication between co-authors to enhance collaboration?

- How might it be possible to influence and measure group effectiveness for groups that meet in order to produce information?

More specifically, it is commonly assumed that a group is a relatively closed and fixed collective, sharing the same goal and engaged in incessant and direct communication (tele-conferencing, electronic blackboards, and electronic mail). But in the case of cooperative multimedia editing these conditions are not satisfied so a range of new problems is posed.

It is important to investigate what each co-author needs to know from the others. A cooperative multimedia editing system must support the retrieval of information stored by, or concerning, other co-authors, perhaps unknown, in another work context, perhaps also unknown. Thus direct and indirect and distributed as well as collective modes of interaction within the group must be possible.

It is necessary to know how group members interrelate and combine their different strategies, reference concepts and partial knowledge, as well as how the specific functional requirements and constraints of a cooperative effort affect the pattern of cooperation. The reasons that move people to engage in cooperative work, in particular in cooperative multimedia editing, and the knowledge required in cooperative as opposed to individual editing are still partially unknown.

Designing cooperative multimedia editing systems can have pitfalls. While the system may be designed to match the current structure of the labour processes, it should not be forgotten that a change in the (use of the) technology induces a change in the structure of the labour process. A framework must be developed for predicting the forms of cooperation and organisation in the course of multimedia technology introduction. This requires an integrative perspective that takes account of the interaction among complex factors, e.g. group structure, media used, group processes and group outcomes.

This work is an evolution of, and strongly based on, the PhD work of the author developed at the Technical University of Darmstadt under the supervision of Prof. Dr. h. c. Dr.-Ing. José Encarnação. The work has been corrected and evaluated also by Dr. Lars Kjelldahl from the KTH Stockholm. The titel of the this PhD thesys was "A framework and architecture for studying the effects of multimedia in cooperative multimedia editing effectiveness".

My first thanks to Prof. J. Encarnação who showed the way and gave the spirit to this work. Thanks for the opportunities, help and incentive. Special thanks are due to Christoph Hornung, Bernhard Tritsch, Adérito Marcos. My very personal gratitude to Belle. Also my best acknowledgements to Sylvia Wilbur, Hannes Lubich and Mike Jäger. I also appreciate the support of Próspero dos Santos, my parents, my mano and Fernanda, Joana and Rainer. I also which to thank the students Sofia Vieira, Georgios Boikos, Zhu Leping, Oliver Eichhorn, Roland Worsch, José Rossa, Norbert Ulmer, Simin Zolfaghari, Rui Guerreiro and Fernando Lobo, not forgetting Elfried Fitschen, Salvador Clavé, Kaisa Väänänen, Jaromir Likavec, Dragana Likavec, Silvia Scherer, Susanne Wurster, Joaquim Madeira, Thomas Kehrer, José-Maria Peiró, Jozé Rugelj, Erik Andriessen, Jeroen Van der Velden, Roland Hjerppe, Erland Jungert, Eevi Beck and Luis Lucas. Finally, thanks to all my colleagues at the House of the Computer Graphics and to J. Dodsworth from Springer-Verlag for the proof-reading.

This work was financially supported by a JNICT CIENCIA schcolarship (BD/1736/91-IA), by the Fraunhofer Institute for Computer Graphics (FhG-IGD), ABB, DEC, ATLAS Elektronik, Vulkan Verbund, the European Commission DEDICATED project (DELTA program) and DAAd.

Darmstadt, April 1995   Adelino Santos

For my wonderful future wife who has been supporting me during this work...
Belle Wünschmann

Table of Contents

Table of Contents

Chapter 1

The Big Bang

"We honour creativity in our culture, especially that of the individual genius, but creativity is as much a group and social affair as an individual one."

Multimedia communication is a recent technical innovation. Until now, to produce a document or to consult together, the authors had to meet face-to-face. Other common forms are the use of FAX, telephone or e-mail. The problem with these is that either they use the vision sense but have the disadvantage of using just a one-way channel, or they use a two-way channel but do not have the advantages of vision. Having a two-way channel with vision/talk/write would be a great advantage. In this sense with a microphone, a camera, a screen to display the camera images and a speaker to reproduce the audio on each side of the communication channel, one could achieve this two-way vision/talk/write paradigm. The camera communication would enable each of the interlocutors to see the other one's environment, the microphone system would enable the communication of audio and the computer would enable the written communication. An integrated use of these various communication media, such as video, audio, text and brainstorming graphics, is necessary to achieve a higher index of user participation and a broader information bandwidth.

The term cooperative multimedia editing is used to designate the set of concepts and tools which allow the members of a group to have synchronous and asynchronous access to a single information object. Group members can see all changes to the objects and are also able to edit them. Concurrent access is done over a network (local or not). The tools can be used to assist interactions that are either face-to-face or remote. One of the critical features of the tools is that they make available to the group a single object (of whatever medium) that is the focus of the collaboration. There must be a common concept on which the group members can work either by reading its contents or by making changes to it via the edit functions provided. This singleness is often achieved through a range of complex architectures which use various mechanisms to maintain an illusion of a single work object.

We see multimedia as an important technology that facilitates work in desktop presentations, cooperative work and training, teaching and communication in general. It modifies the way people learn or, in broader terms, communicate. These modifications tend to increase the speed, amount and accuracy of communication. Increasing the modalities with which people can communicate enables people to choose the communicating method that best fits their needs. The key to multimedia is the ability to link different types of information. Usually the use of interactive multimedia enables the integration of several forms of information with friendly and straightforward control over the focused topics, the media used and the level of detail presented. In a typical multimedia application, one is able to write/read text, integrate graphics, incorporate animation sequences and moving graphics on the screen, record/use screen sections, record/use sounds or a piece of a digitised speech or music. By linking computer based information with audio, still or full-motion video, camera imaging, animation, graphic features, text and high-resolution graphics one can get a multimedia system of unparalleled impact. Several factors drive together the media that compose most of the multimedia applications. Examples are the technology improvements of the last years, namely the dropping prices of boards, chips, graphic monitors, storage media, etc., the increasing marketing profile for graphics/video/audio integrating applications, the growing importance of distributed and networked processing, the development of more powerful interfaces and input devices and the devising of compression algorithms which make storage and transmission of multimedia data economical.

Group support and effectiveness involves the techniques to support group work and to enhance its effectiveness. Computer-supported groups are, generally, project-oriented (goal-oriented) with important tasks and tight deadlines. The group members may be present in the same room or they may be attending an electronic meeting at which not all members are present in the same place or at the same time. Sometimes computer-supported groups are permanent and formal groups; other situations require ad-hoc groups with a finite lifetime and other kinds of properties. The group interaction might be formal or informal, spontaneous or planned, structured or unstructured, which leads to a large number of possible approaches and applications types in the area of computer support for groups.

Although computers have been used to support team efforts, the emerging concept of computer-supported groups differs from traditional computer support concepts. Many computer systems, such as time-sharing or networked systems, are common place and only support loose aggregations of users without any support for the connection among them (cognitive, common data, simultaneous or synchronised actions). Each user is seen as a discrete unit without any semantic connection to the others. Computer-supported groups introduce a new dimension and a new necessity: software designed specifically for groups.

A significant portion of time spent within organisations is spent working or trying to work in groups (see table below). The estimates range from 60% to 70% for managers. Stefik (see [Stefik et al. 87]) refers to studies that indicate that office workers can spend up to 70% of their time in meetings. A recent German study (see [Hymowitz 88, Applegate 91]) determined that managers spend 40% of their 59-hour working week on communication. Their detailed analysis yielded the following results:

Work activity type	Time	Work activity type	Time
Informal meetings	19 (%)	Official meetings	8 (%)
Telephone	13 (%)	Incoming mail	8 (%)
Reading documents	11 (%)	Outgoing mail	7 (%)
Preparing documents	11 (%)	Other activities	23 (%)

A large proportion of time is spent in information production either individually or within a group: 18% (preparing documents, outgoing mail) of the time relates directly to document production; and 26% (classic informal and official meetings) directly to group work and indirectly to document production. The majority of the communication time is used for coordination: coordination of people working together towards goals they would not achieve alone. Thus the time spent in group work makes group effectiveness (for example, through computer-supported cooperation) a key issue. This just shows the time aspect of document production and group effectiveness. Other aspects than this one can be used to measure the effectiveness of a group, e.g. the quality of the outcomes or the physical resources spent.

It is relatively easy to find different taxonomies in the literature classifying cooperative work and multimedia. Nevertheless, most of them fail to integrate the cooperation notion conveniently with the multimedia notion. Also, they do not incorporate notions such as time, multimedia presentation streams, modes of media presentation, mode of cooperation or media used in face-to-face and remote meetings. The two taxonomies in Figs. 1.1 and 1.2 incorporate the relevant notions of this work and their relations with other important concepts.

Media-oriented Taxonomy:
Document Contents and Communication

In Fig. 1.1 we show a non-exhaustive taxonomy of media for documents and communication classifying four of the most common media, namely text, graphics, audio, and video. From this taxonomy one could choose the set of media to be included in a system specifying the type of contents of the documents. The most common media in classic documents are text and still graphics. Nevertheless, in richer documents we can have textual and graphical content that speaks, shows animated sequences and helps to manipulate mathematical expressions.

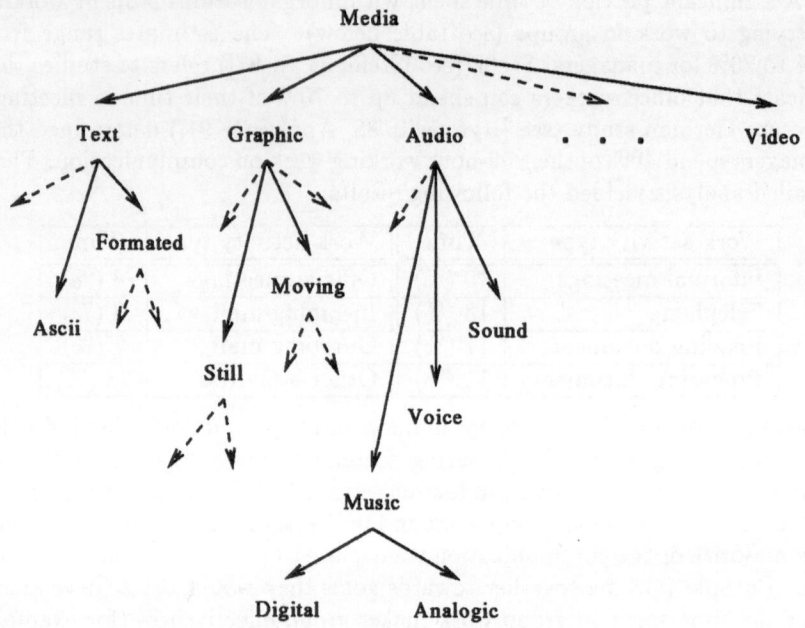

Fig. 1.1: A non-exhaustive media-oriented taxonomy. Every dashed line represents what falls outside the scope of this work

On the other hand, from the taxonomy one could also choose the set of media for use as communication channels. These are to be made available to the group members for communication. Traditional examples of communication media in meetings include face-to-face, text and still graphics. Nevertheless, audio and video have the capacity to convey very rich information within the group and are privileged communication channels.

Activity-oriented Taxonomy: Cooperative Multimedia Editing

In Fig. 1.2 we present an activity-oriented taxonomy to classify work starting from its broadest meaning to the specific kind of activity named cooperative multimedia editing. When decision-makers are faced with genuinely important tasks, it is likely that they will assign those tasks to groups. The reason can be that one individual would not be able to handle the task alone (e.g. formulating of a new tax policy requires many kinds of knowledge and skills) or the assumption that the added human resources available in a group will lead to a higher quality of output. This constitutes the classification of the broad notion of work into group work and individual work (step 1) using the number of individuals that perform the work as classification criteria.

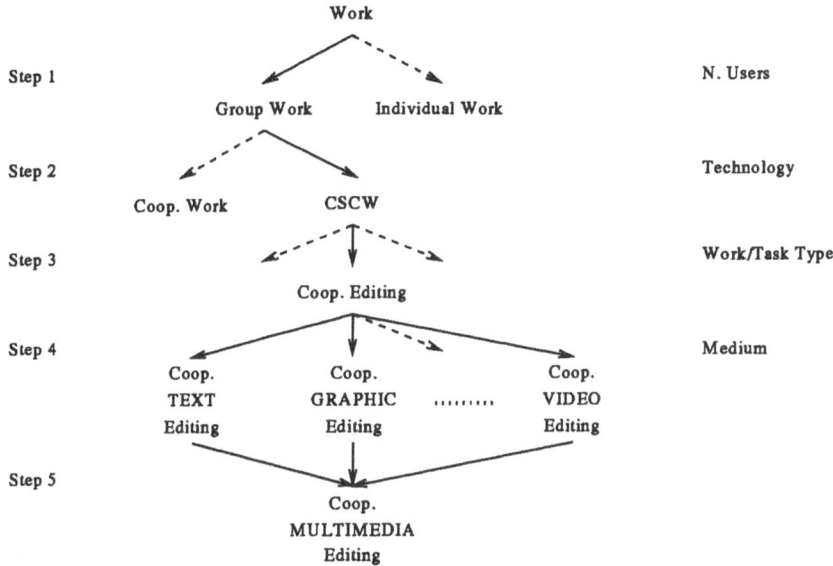

Fig. 1.2: An activity-oriented taxonomy. From the broad notion of work to cooperative multimedia editing. The right column represents the classifying criteria of each step

Advances in technical capabilities for supporting group communication and interaction, together with organisational focus on groups, have stimulated a significant increase in research and industry effort on the use of the information technology to support group work. This includes support for both synchronous and asynchronous communication in small and large groups in one or more face-to-face or geographically dispersed meeting situations (step 2). This area of research is termed computer-supported cooperative work (CSCW), and the commercial products or prototype systems that arise from the concepts here developed is called groupware. The aims of researchers in this field are to describe the general features of collaborative work and the specific details of particular kinds of collaboration, to create technological systems that will improve the quality and efficiency of collaborative work, to foster kinds of collaboration that would be impossible without advanced communication and computer support and to assess the impact of these technologies on individuals, groups and organisations.

CSCW has expanded and already has subdisciplines. Using as classification mechanism the type of cooperative work (type of group task) to be supported by the technology, we devise several subdisciplines (step 3). Examples are group decision support systems, project management software, calendar management for groups, group editing software, computer-supported face-to-face meetings, screen-sharing software, computer conferencing software, information-filtering software, computer-supported video tele-conferences, conversational structuring and computer-supported spontaneous interaction. One of these examples is cooperative editing, in which a group of co-authors cooperatively uses a software editing system to produce information.

Step 4 uses the media as classification criteria to divide cooperative editing. To convey information in conventional documents the most popular and widely used media are text and 2D-graphics. But as information becomes more complex, the media necessary for better expression of ideas range from 3D-graphics to video. These are used to convey other types of information, usually more condensed and in more user-friendly formats.

We want here to move ahead and study the characteristics of the cooperative editing process upon a multimedia document (step 5). Cooperative multimedia editing is the process of using multimedia applications to create multimedia materials within a group. It uses a wide variety of tools, from the more familiar text editor or desktop publishing application to tools for capturing and manipulating video images or editing audio files. It can be performed on several media: e.g. voice, music, still images, motion video, graphics and text. Over time, everyone involved in business communication will probably have some level of multimedia editing capability.

The concept of integrated multimedia can be combined with the concept of cooperative editing in two ways. One is the enrichment of the contents of documents that can be produced, enabling the so-called multimedia documents. Another involves the use of several media to facilitate the cooperation process, namely by supporting communication.

Chapter 2

State-of-the-art and Terminology

> *"If a multimedia CSCW system or technology requires more effort to use than a single-user single-medium one, users will be very likely to reject it."*

In this chapter we would like to review the current status of the technology and available applications in the fields of multimedia processing, multimedia communication, computer-supported cooperative work, cooperative multimedia editing and usability studies.

In Sect. 2.1, we touch two fields of multimedia processing: audio and video processing. Audio processing is the facility allowing someone to create, edit or delete sequences of sounds. Audio processing helps to remove the communication barriers between humans and computers. Video processing systems are software systems that allow users to capture video images, paint them, and output them. These systems can mix colours, balance chrominance and luminance, mix recorded video with artificially generated images, use masking and cut-out features and so on. Using a video paint system integrated with a multimedia system allows, for example, the integration of audio and text in video images. One could record diverse component media separately so that they would be independently editable.

Communication issues are dealt in Sect. 2.2. Nowadays people use mostly letters, telephone, FAX, telex and e-mail to communicate. The problem with these ways of communication is that either they use the vision sense but have the disadvantage of using just a one-way channel, or they use a two-way channel (such as telephone) but do not have the advantages of vision. Having a two-way channel with vision/talk/write would be a great advantage. With a microphone, a camera, a screen to display the camera images, and a speaker to reproduce the audio on each side of the communication channel, this two-way vision/talk/write paradigm can be achieved. The video communication enables each of the interlocutors to see the other one's environment. The audio system enables communication of voices and the computer enables written communication.

Section 2.3 reviews notions necessary to understand the framework and model conceptualised in Chap. 3.

Recent evolution has stimulated an increase in research and industry effort on the use of the information technology to support coordination, collaboration and group decision making. This includes support for both synchronous and asynchronous communication in small and large groups in one or more face-to-face or geographically dispersed meeting situations. This area is termed Computer-Supported Cooperative Work (CSCW) and the commercial products or prototype systems that arise from it are called groupware. Groupware systems can be used in formulation of corporate strategy, consultative medical diagnosis, collaborative scientific research, design of products in the manufacturing industry (e.g. car, ship, hardware products), advertising campaigns, jointly authored magazine articles. The central image underlying these examples is one of individuals working together to produce or manipulate information and they illustrate that group work occurs in a myriad of tasks and settings. These groups are searching for tools that will help them perform their jobs.

In Sect. 2.4 we explain that a (multimedia) editing system is a software application that allows authors to easily combine different media (graphics, text, video, audio, animation and so on) into a single multimedia document. A cooperative (multimedia) editing system (or authoring system) allows the members of a group to have synchronous and asynchronous access to a single information object. Group members can see all changes to the objects and may be able to edit it. Concurrent access is done over a network.

The last Sect. of this chapter deals with the problem of evaluating cooperation support and multimedia communication prototype systems. Today, no one can predict in any detail the nature of the transformations that computer technology will bring for our life, but one aspect that will be certainly affected is the way we communicate. The functions and impact of collaboration support are still poorly understood. Critical information (e.g. who uses it and for what purposes) is lacking, and the social significance is controversial. For instance, access to electronic communication may change the flow of information within organisations, altering status relations and organisation hierarchy.

2.1 Multimedia Processing

To work in multimedia is to recognise that knowledge does not reside privately in individual minds, or text books, or journals, or libraries, or laboratories, or databases or life experiences. Knowledge resides in a space that covers and encompasses all of these. Indeed information is not static, and everyone in the community of persons who work with some or all of the above facets of knowledge has to have access and give access to it. Everyone in this community shares the responsibility, and has the chance, of testing knowledge and adding to it.

A medium is a means by which information is perceived, expressed, stored or transmitted. This term is very general and sometimes ambiguous and should mostly be used in expressions such as perception medium, representation medium, presentation medium. Otherwise we write medium refering to the last (when an accurate terminology is not required). A perception medium is the nature of information as perceived by the user. Examples are speech, music, text, drawings, moving scens, and so on. A representation medium is the type of data which defines the nature of the information as described in its coded form. Examples are for text: ASCII, EBCDIC, for audio: CCITT G711, MIDI, MPEG-Audio, for still images: JPEG, PostScript. A presentation medium is the type of physical means which is used to reproduce information to the user (output device) or to acquire information from the user (input device).

Media objects are entities that encapsulate the specific processing and synchronisation associated with the acquisition, handling and restitution of representation media. Examples are audio, text, fixed or moving video. Media objects can be basic or composite. Basic media objects are units of media representation. A basic medium object corresponds to a single instance of a representation medium. Composite objects are constructed by the composition of several other media objects (basic or composite), called component objects. The behaviour of a composite object is derived from a composition of the behaviours of its component objects.

Multimedia can be defined as the property of handling several types of representation media. In general, multimedia objects are composite media objects handling several types of representation media (or several instances of the same representation media). Multimedia communication is the transport of data between entities (processes or users) that can be co-located or not, consisting of more than one medium.

There are two classes of synchronisation within a multimedia framework: serial synchronisation and parallel synchronisation. Serial synchronisation determines the rate at which events must occur within a single data stream; this includes the rate at which audio information is processed, or video information is fetched. Parallel synchronisation determines the relative scheduling of separate synchronisation streams. In most non-trivial multimedia applications, each stream will have a serial synchronisation requirement and a parallel relationship with other streams. Another distinction is between point and continuous synchronisation. Point synchronisation requires only that a single point of a block coincides with a single point of another. Continuous synchronisation can be managed by the applications layer, while continuous synchronisation will need to be managed by a device controller or a high-performance, low-overhead portion of the operating system. There are also different levels of precision. Stereo audio channels must be synchronised very closely (within 1 to 0.1 millisecond), because perception of the stereo effect is based on minimal phase differences. A lip-synchronous audio track to go with a video movie requires a precision of 10 to 100 milliseconds. Subtitles only require a 0.1 to 1 second of imprecision. Sometimes even longer deviations are acceptable (background music, slides).

Multimedia data is isochronous in nature, i.e. each media stream is a sequence of finite sized samples (such as video frames or audio samples) which convey meaning only when presented continuously in time (unlike a textual object, for which spatial continuity is sufficient). In addition, there may be the need for synchronisation between multimedia streams. Therefore, retrieval of media streams must proceed so as to ensure both continuity of each of the media streams and the synchronisation between them.

Synchronisation is the set of techniques for specifying, representing and enforcing temporal relationships between media streams. It can be seen from several perspectives: the synchronisation of a speaker's lips between a audio and a video stream, or the synchronisation of several data streams (possibly belonging to several media) done by a operating system or an application. Several approaches to this problem have been taken. Petri-nets-based models can be used for formally describing synchronisation requirements among media streams, and also developed synchronisation mechanisms for enforcing these requirements at the time of retrieval. Other proposals present a two-level scheme for media communication, in which temporal relationships between media units can be specified at a logical data level and implemented at a physical data level. The most used techniques include mechanisms using the synchronisation marker concept for indication of synchronisation points. Some approaches worked to integrate the synchronisation mechanisms into the OSI model.

Synchronicity can be characterised together with other terms, such as synchronisation or synchronous, by the simultaneous or at least coordinated input (capture) transport, process, store or display of information from more than one media stream (see [Tritsch et al. 92]). Asynchronous and asynchronicity can be defined by the failing of synchronicity or synchronisation. If the data is not dealt with simultaneously (for example e-mail) we have asynchronicity. An important aspect in the distinction between asynchronicity and synchronous is not in the speed it can happen (otherwise a very fast e-mail could appear synchronous to a user) but in the warranty it can happen in a determined time constraint (then a very fast e-mail cannot be synchronous). Isochronous processing refers to just one media stream, and it can be defined as the synchronisation between a media stream and the time dimension. It is invoked to guarantee that a media stream is input, transported, processed, stored or displayed correctly in time.

2.1.1   Audio Processing

Audio processing is the facility that enables someone to create, edit, or delete sounds or sequences of sounds. We can divide this theme into voice processing and music processing.

Although we no longer use switches to communicate with computers, computer input has been more a barrier than a gate. Voice processing offers the possibility of interfacing with computers using our best-developed communication skill - speech (see Sect. 2.2). The advantage of audio processing is that it helps to remove the communication barriers between humans and computers. Integrating this kind of processing in multimedia applications will bring one of the most important goals of all multimedia systems - communication, closer. Speech processing is a sequence of transformations that converts an analogue speech signal into a compact yet informative digital representation of speech. A microphone converts the changes that the speech causes in air pressure to voltage variations. The system samples these variations and digitises them using an A/D converter. The sequence of numbers thus created is called the digital wave form which contains many redundancies (a 5-second utterance may produce up to 100 000 numbers). Digital-signal-processing techniques (reduction techniques) are then applied to reduce redundancy and enhance the salient features of speech. Common reduction techniques include filter banks and fast Fourier transformations. After these processing steps, the speech can be recorded as sound, recorded as text, or interpreted as natural language meaningful utterances.

Nowadays we have more than the boring beeps and buzzes of the early microcomputers. The invention of MIDI (Music Instrument Digital Interface) enabled many advances in this field. MIDI is a protocol for sending digital information over serial lines between electronic musical instruments and equipment, including computers. This information includes note on, note off, speed of keystroke, pressure applied after the keystroke, pitch bend, modulation wheel, foot pedal, and sound changes. MIDI enables the writing of multimedia applications that take advantage of its ability to interface synthesisers directly with personal computers. Today there are five categories of audio software: Sequencers, Editors/librarians, Notation programs, Pattern generators and Film score utilities.

A sequencer is a program that records the events and gestures of a musical performance. The sequencer can play back the instructions to the appropriate synthesiser or audio module, telling it exactly when to trigger its sounds. Unlike tape, the audio performance never degrades in quality because the audio is always first-generation. Dedicated music sequencers had existed prior to MIDI, but it was only when the power of microcomputers with graphics was added to the MIDI network that sequencing packages developed into intuitive music-making programs.

The graphics editing tools include the same kinds of cut-and-paste, copy, insert, and delete commands that can be found on any word processor. The analogy is simple and good: music sequencers let the user manipulate and manage music as a word processor lets the user manipulate text. Voice-editing software displays all of a synthesiser's internal voice parameters simultaneously. Editors can depict complex voice parameters graphically far better than the built-in LCDs of the synthesiser. A librarian is simply a database for storing and retrieving sounds.

Notation programs are used to produce music notation. The objective of such programs is that a performance can be played and instantly print out a music manuscript in perfect standard musical notation.

The necessity of incorporating music into multimedia environments will force applications to integrate music with video, graphics, and other media, but we think that the basic music software tools - sequencer, voice editor, librarian, notator and so on - are already mature.

A multimedia system can embody sampling/synthesising/sequencing/music editing software to enable a user to control and manipulate samples to record sounds, synthesisers to create new sounds, or simple music instruments to record and play back music. With such software tools the user can include professional audio in an animation sequence or video sequence, use a music editor to compose new pieces, or use a voice editor to compose speeches. Now a new world of polyphonic, multitimbral, multitrack digital music systems is available for most users.

In the X-Windows platform using SUN SPARCstations 2 or 10 and SGI Indigo there is no need for extra audio hardware. The programmers have the possibility of using the audio libraries that use the standard hardware. In the SGI Indigo workstations the audio has stereo quality, 16 bits per sample. In the SPARCstation 2 workstations the audio has mono (telephone) quality, 8 bits per sample and in the SPARCstation 10 workstations, stereo quality, 16 bits per sample.

In the MS-Windows platform a number of cards that provide audio and/or MIDI interface are available on the market. One of them, Sound Blaster Pro, seems to have become a market standard.

2.1.2   Video Processing

Video processing systems (also called titling systems) are computer software systems that allow users to capture video images, paint them, and output them onto video. These systems are becoming more important each day. With these systems one can mix colours, balance chrominance and luminance, mix recorded video with artificially generated colours, use masking and cut-out features and so on. Using such a video paint system integrated within a multimedia system would allow, for example, the integration of audio and text in video images. More complicated would be the introduction of animated titles or video background animation. Also the mapping of graphical textures in video characters as letters, objects, or persons would be an available tool.

One could record diverse component media separately so that they would be independently editable.

In the X-Windows platform products such as VideoPix IndigoVideo, XVideo, RGB View Video, VideoPhile are available.

In the MS-Windows platform products such as Miro Movie, FAST Screen-Machine, Matrox Studio, FluentStreams, Personal Producer, VideoMaker+, VideoScene Master 100 are available.

2.2 Multimedia Communication

The past forty years have seen dramatic advances in information and telecommunication technologies, and the widespread adoption of these technologies bears the best testimony to the advent of the "information society". In the western world there has been a shift from traditional economy sectors to services in general and to information handling in particular. According to a study launched by the Commission of the European Community, telecommunication will be a driving force in the European economy by the beginning of the next millennium, with an annual estimated growth rate of 8%, as compared to e.g. the car industry, with only 2% (see Fig. 2.1).

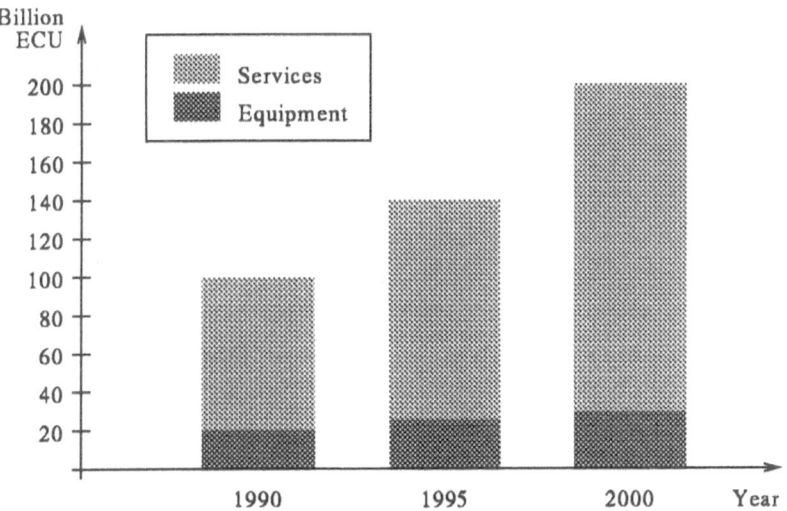

Fig. 2.1: The tele-communication market in western Europe

Personalised services will be offered in the sense that easy access to networked services will be enabled independently of the location of the user. Service presentation and user-friendliness will become an important marketing instrument for service providers, and users will have the opportunity of tailoring, individual services supporting individual applications. Furthermore, the trade-off between common presentation and product differentiation for services and terminals will have to be identified and developed.

Nowadays people use letters, telephone, FAX, telex, e-mail, and so on to communicate. The problem with these ways of communication is that either they use the vision sense but have the disadvantage of using just a one-way channel, or they use a two-way channel (such as telephone) but do not have the advantages of vision. Having a two-way channel with vision/talk/write would be a great advantage. With a microphone, a camera, a screen to display the camera images, and a speaker to reproduce the sound on each side of the communication channel, one could achieve this two-way vision/talk/write paradigm. The camera communication would enable each of the interlocutors to see the other one's environment. The microphone system would enable the communication of sounds, namely voices. The computer would enable the written communication.

The communication requirements which should be met in multimedia communication systems and cooperative systems are similar to others that already exist on the market. These requirements could be fulfilled by two types of networks that are currently available and sufficiently wide spread over most universities and industry - Ethernet as a Local Area Network (LAN) and Integrated Services Digital Network (ISDN) as a Wide Area Network (WAN).

Both Ethernet and ISDN have moved rapidly from the experimental stages to commercial availability. The reasons for this are the fundamental trends in the data processing industry: the rapid move from mainframes to smaller, cheaper and more flexible processing units and networking of these.

An attempt to align the definition and classification of several network types and selected service attributes is shown in the following table (depicting Transfer Modes vs. Connection-oriented/Connectionless networks.

	Transfer Mode			
	Circuit	Packet	Frame	Cell
Connection Oriented	Telephone Telex ISDN	X.25 (virtual circuit)	Frame-Relay	B-ISDN (ATM)
Connectionless	—	TCP/IP	Ethernet Token Ring Token Bus FDDI	DQDB MAN

We will now examine the characteristics of each of the different types of network.

Circuit-switched networks: dedicate a fixed part of the network resource for each call. They offer a high degree of transparency to information format within a fixed bandwidth and require the user to set up each call which can be a problem in some applications. The main characteristics are: Transport capacity is negotiated; Predictable performance; Resources are under-utilised when user is quiet; Transfer rate is equal to circuit bandwidth; Inefficiency of connection set-up time; Originator must know the address of destination.

Packet-switched networks: was most popular when digital techniques were first introduced, because it allowed network resources to be allocated just when required, used the same information format for virtual call set-up and for transport of user information and provided a standardised protocol which allowed many different types of terminal inter work. Bit-rate transparency was a key factor in permitting this inter working. The main characteristics are: Transport capacity is determined by access rate and network occupancy; Less predictable performance; Greater potential for resource sharing; Transfer rate is network dependent; Fast virtual call set-up; Originator must know the address of destination; Address processing at each switch limits throughput.

Frame relay networks: can be thought of as an evolution of packet-switched networks. Throughput has been greatly increased by transfer of some of the functions from the terminal equipment which can handle them more efficiently. The main characteristics are: Transport capacity is negotiated; Predictable performance; Potential for resource sharing; Transfer rate is network dependent; Inefficiency of connection set-up time; Originator must know the address of destination.

Connectionless networks: have as major advantage the fact that the originator of a message does not have to know the location of its recipient and does not have the overhead of setting up a call. The disadvantage is that all information has to be sent to all networks which places a heavy burden on network resources in large networks. The main characteristics are: Network can be saturated by heavy users; Unpredictable performance; Full resource sharing; Transfer at full network rate; No connection set-up overhead; Originator does not need to know the address of destination; Inherent point-to-multi-point; Security issues for multi-user networks.

2.3 Computer-supported Cooperative Work

Computer-supported groups are, generally, project-oriented (or goal-oriented) with important tasks and tight deadlines. The group members may be present in the same room or they may be attending an electronic meeting at which the other members are not present in the same place or at the same time. Sometimes computer-supported groups are permanent and formal groups; other situations require ad hoc groups with a finite lifetime and other kinds of properties. The group interaction might be formal or informal, spontaneous or planned, structured or unstructured (see Chap. 3 and [Johansen 89] for additional definitions), which leads to a large number of possible approaches and applications types in the area of computer support for groups.

Work is a "physical or mental effort directed towards doing or making something". But, more important for this research is the notion of cooperative work - work processes that are related as to content, that is, processes relating to the production of a particular service, product or type of products (see Sects. 3.1, 4.2 and 4.4). This is a far more specific concept than social interaction in the system of work in general. It refers to the concept of production, which means it does not apply to every work-related interaction. The definition is as general as possible, and in fact this term is usually defined or used in a rather general and neutral form. We do not presuppose any specific organisational setting or form. The concept does not imply a specific degree of regularity, nor does it imply such notions as face-to-face communication or group cohesion. A specific corporation may have multiple cooperative work processes with no mutual interferences, and these may cross corporate boundaries. In the phrase "cooperative work" cooperation refers to production, i.e. cooperative work stops existing where consumption begins (a group of people reading a document is not cooperating). Furthermore, though we do not presuppose any organisational setting or form, an organisational form is needed i.e. the cooperative relations must be established deliberately, as opposed to accidentally.

Place \ Time	Same	Different
Same	Meeting Environments	Team Work Work Shifts
Different	Tele-, Video-, Desktop- Conferencing	Electronic Mail Computer Conferences Collaborative Writing Workflow Management

Fig. 2.2: The Johansen's Time/Place matrix

Advances in technical capabilities for supporting group communication and information, together with organisational focus on groups, have stimulated a significant increase in research and industry effort on the use of information technology to support group work. This includes support for both synchronous and asynchronous communication in small and large groups in one or more face-to-face or geographically dispersed meeting situations. This area of research is termed computer-supported cooperative work (CSCW), and the commercial products or prototype systems that arise from the concepts here developed is called groupware. Taking the previous definition of cooperative work, if this is supported by technology to enable multiple individuals to work together to solve one or more common problems, then we attain the term CSCW (see [Applegate 91]). To give an example of CSCW, one area of CSCW research that has received increasing attention over the past five years is the support of "face-to-face" meetings in electronic meeting environments with multimedia communication channels. The importance of meetings - a fact of life in most organisations - is expected to increase as we move toward team-based organisation designs. It has been estimated that managers and knowledge workers spend between 30% and 80% of their time in meetings (see [Hymowitz 88]).

Time Place	Same	Different (predictable)	Different (unpredictable)
Same	Meeting Environments	Work Shifts	Team Work
Different (predictable)	Tele-, Video-, Desktop- Conferencing	Electronic Mail	Collaborative Writing
Different (unpredictable)	Broadcast Seminars	Computer Conferences News Groups	Workflow Management

Fig. 2.3: Another version of the Johansen Time/Place matrix

Considering a Time/Place perspective, there are four sets of circumstances that lend themselves to CSCW technology support (see [Johansen 88]): same time/same place; same time/different place; different time/same place and different time/different place collaboration. These can be represented on a 2×2 matrix that spans over time and place to classify CSCW applications (see Fig. 2.2). In a fully integrated CSCW organisation support system, the intersection of these four perspectives would enable any time/any place col-

laboration (see Figs. 2.2). Following the same perspective Grudin specified
the matrix further to achieve the 3×3 matrix of Fig. 2.3.

2.3.1   Approaches to Computer-supported Cooperative Work

Recognising the links between disciplines such as computer science, office automation, human factors, management science, organisational science, sociol-
ogy, anthropology, and psychology, Irene Greif and Paul Cashman organised
a workshop in 1984. Although the workshop was only a small affair, it con-
vinced them that the topic was worth pursuing, and they initiated the first
CSCW conference in Austin, Texas in 1986. The conference was a success,
and since then a substantial CSCW research community has been established.
Every second year there is a CSCW conference in USA (1988 - Portland, 1990
- Los Angeles, 1992 - Toronto) and in Europe (1989 - Gatwick, 1991 - Amsterdam, 1993 - Milan). Here we describe a set of possible approaches to
cooperative support for groups based on the taxonomy of Fig. 2.4.

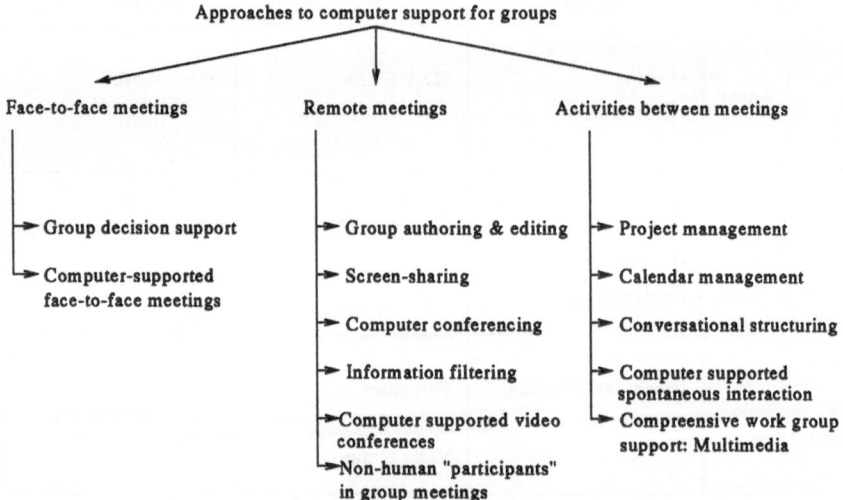

Fig. 2.4: Approaches to computer support for groups according to the time
frame in which the support is provided

2.3.1.1   Group Decision Support Systems

Decision support systems have gradually emerged and are now heavily used
within many companies. The concept was introduced as long ago as in 1988
and is defined as the use of computers to (see also [Johansen 89]):

- Assist managers in their decision processes in semi-structured tasks;

- Support, rather than replace, managerial judgement;

- Improve the effectiveness of decision making.

Extending these concepts to computer-supported groups we get the concept of group decision support systems (GDSS). GDSS have been in use in limited ways for almost twenty years. Kraemer, in [Kraemer et al. 88], conducted a survey of such systems and concluded that, in spite of years of attempts "...the field of GDSS is as yet not well developed, even as a concept". There are isolated examples, but there is little industry success to report. However, research activities are increasing and the techniques for decision support are becoming both more powerful and less obtrusive for users.

GDSS, while plentiful for individuals, often lack the flexibility needed for group applications in business. Furthermore, formal procedures for decision making are often discouraged by "real business people"; significant changes in perceptions and procedures may be necessary. Conference rooms may need to be adapted to allow for GDSS, and this is likely to be expensive. Most companies are used to conference room expenditures that only include such inexpensive items as overhead and slide projectors, or perhaps a microphone.

In most organisations, group decision making goes on at both high and low levels, and encompasses strategic, operational and technical issues. There is considerable evidence that group decision making is often suboptimal, not only because of the cognitive limitations of the decision makers, but because of difficulties in group dynamics that arise during the evaluation and selection of alternatives. GDSS differ from each other on the cost, number of users that can be accommodated, whether users must be co-located or can be geographically dispersed, and the sort of support provided for the group's activities. Usually, the elements of group decision support system technology are an appropriately designed facility, hardware, software and a trained facilitator. Examples of a system in this area are Collaborative Management Room (University of Arizona), Decision Conference (Decision and Design Inc.), GroupSystems/TeamFocus (Ventana Inc./IBM), SIBYL (MIT) and VisionQuest (CTC).

2.3.1.2 Project Management Software - Team Conscience

Work groups have obvious and often pressing needs for task planning and coordination. Specialised software can help them plan what needs to be done, track their progress in reaching goals, and coordinate activities of individual group members. The big issue with project management software is to find a system that all group members will use. Usually a group has better things to do during the precious and most of the times expensive time of a meeting than keeping record of deadlines, schedules, task breakdowns and tasks to accomplish.

Project management software is becoming common on personal computers, and also increasingly good. Some systems even include limited artificial intelligence capabilities that allow for internal judgements about progress or lack of it.

Any approach to project management must be used by all group members in order to be valuable. Project management software must be compatible enough with the styles of the group members to allow this participation to occur. This will be tough for software designers, because the needs and styles of work groups varies greatly (see [Johansen 89]). Examples of software in this area are COSMOS (British Telecom), MasterPlan (Unipress), MicroTrak (SoftTrak), PMS-80 (Pinnell Engineering Inc.), TACTS (University München), Ultra Planner (Productivity Solutions), and Workflo (FileNet).

2.3.1.3   Calendar Management for Groups

Work groups need to coordinate calendars with each other and perhaps others outside the group. Unfortunately, the implementation of calendar systems is not as straightforward as the concept. Many people are reluctant to use computer-based calendars, often with good reason.

Usually calendars have a set of role definitions and a specification of which roles can be assumed by different users. The systems provide a default set of role definitions so that owners do not have to describe all roles from scratch. These defaults reflect some reasonable expectation about how individuals might wish to control access to their calendars. An example is that someone with the role of *secretary* can confirm and cancel appointments on the owner's behalf. Members of the *public* role can only make proposals for appointments, which must be confirmed or rejected by either the owner or the secretary. The *public* role can only see blocks of time marked BUSY, and members of the owner's (manager) *team* can see the details of individual appointments.

Electronic calendars have been accepted very slowly within most user communities, especially by those people who have secretaries or assistants who will schedule the meetings for them so they can avoid the hassle. Gradually, however, calendar systems are coming onto the market. On the other side, logistics of group calendar are becoming better understood and the implications are promising (see [Johansen 89]).

One of the worst pitfalls is that the users must designate times that are unavailable and available, with a weighting flexibility. Firstly is hard and time-consuming to find these "time holes" and parameterise them, and then it is necessary to trust that everyone will do the same for their time. As an aspect of project management, group calendars require full participation, which is difficult to achieve in many groups. In addition, people are usually very protective of their personal calendars; they are likely to resist the notion of an electronically accessible tool. Examples can be found in software for offices such as CaLANdar (Microsystems Software Inc.), Calendar Manager (shareware), Calendar Tool (shareware), Clockwise (Phase II Software Corp.), Khronika (EuroPARC), Meeting Maker (ON Technology Inc.), Office Vision (IBM), OnTime (Cambell Services) and WordPerfect Office (WordPerfect Corp.).

2.3.1.4 Group Authoring and Editing Software

One important class of software that is emerging in the area of computer-supported cooperative work is what one might call a group editor, which allows the members of a group to have synchronous and asynchronous access to a single information object. Members can see all changes to the object and may be able to edit it. Concurrent access is done over a network. The editors can be used to assist interactions that are either face-to-face or remote. This contrasts with systems that give the group members asynchronous access to a single object, such as document authoring tools that coordinate comments and changes from a number of co-authors. It also contrasts with the systems consisting of one machine whose display is projected onto a publicly viewable screen, run by a scribe or facilitator (see [Olson et al. 90]).

A number of systems have been built to explore this group editing function. There are two broad classes of such systems. In one class, the group editing function allows true concurrent access by all participants. In a second class of systems, a single-user editor is "groupified" through one of several mechanisms (creating shared access to a single machine's application; individual machines networked with a group machine that one member of the group controls at a time). Systems of the second type allow one person to edit at any given moment, though rapid shifts of control may be possible. In either class, potentially any kind of object could be presented to the group for editing: text, outlines, graphics, spreadsheets, audio and video sequences.

One of the critical features of a group editor is that it makes available to the group a single object (of whatever medium) that is the focus of whatever they are collaborating on. There must be a common concept on which the group members can work either by reading its contents or by making changes to it via the edit functions provided. This singleness is often achieved through a range of complex architectures which use various mechanisms to maintain an illusion of a single work object.

Some editors allow co-authors to edit the object simultaneously. Other group editors provide serial access to the workspace, as if the keyboards and mice were connected octopus style to one machine. Single entry systems allow only one person at a time to enter commands or material. Some systems take inputs on a first come first served priority. Others require each person to indicate by pressing a button that they want "the floor". This explicit control keeps people from producing jumbles of actions from overlapping keystrokes or simultaneous mouse movements. The other freer systems avoid jumbles by social control, asking and giving permission verbally.

At the heart of all group editors is a model of access that is fully public and sharable. But many group editors have explored a variety of different mechanisms for mixing public and private work. Total privacy is achieved when some aspect of the work is available only to one person. From here to fully public information there can be several steps:

- Private view: such that co-authors can view (e.g. scroll) any part of the object on their own. This differs from those below in that the object is not changed or transformed in any way, just looked at from different vantage point.

- Private transformed views: are qualitatively different formats for displaying the object;

- Private workspaces: are unconnected with the shared workspace (e.g. a separate window);

- Private attached objects: are connected to a shared object.

One very general design question is the extent to which features required to support the group use of such editors should be provided as an aspect of the editor itself, as against being left to social control among the participants via one of these other channels. For examples of systems in this area see Sect. 2.4.

2.3.1.5   Computer-supported Face-to-face Meetings

There must be more than one computer in a room and the users must be skilled enough to use the software (this can involve training people who usually do not deal directly with computers). Here the technologies also called electronic meeting support systems (EMSS) are used to support group process, coordination and communication in face-to-face meetings, as well as geographically dispersed meetings. The majority of these technologies have been developed in research environments connected with universities or business research environments. This kind of software builds on the familiar notion of face-to-face meetings.

A typical scenario is the production of a report on which each of the group members has been working in private. All meet in a room with appropriate computer support for a final preparatory meeting. There is a semi-circular table with five computer screens connected together to a big wall-display screen. Members work privately at their workstations or publicly, displaying their work to all the group through the wall-display screen. When they leave the room, they leave with a common "group memory" of what has occurred and what steps will occur next.

The CoLab environment (see [Stefik et al. 87]) at Xerox Palo Alto research Centre (PARC) is already beyond the stage in the example above.

They have been working on this prototype since 1987. Several other commercial attempts to develop more limited systems have met with little commercial success. The technology for face-to-face meeting support is almost there, but it is difficult and expensive to assemble. Integration of the hardware components is complex, and the software, in most cases, is only available in research laboratory settings. Examples of systems within this approach are CoLab (XeroxPARC), Capture Lab (MCC), COPE (University of Strathclyde), Electronic Meeting Room (IBM), GroupSystems/TeamFocus (Ventana/IBM) and Project NICK (MCC).

2.3.1.6 Screen-sharing Software

This approach builds directly on personal computer and workstation use: anything that can be displayed on one screen could be usefully shared with another person's screen. This has been labelled as Xerox PARC as WYSIWIS (What You See Is What I See - see Sect. 4.1.2 and [Stefik 86]). Nowadays, most of the systems have WYSIWIS in one way or the other. The early steps were taken in areas where, in addition to explicit communication (telephone, video channel, and so on), the users would exchange ideas about something on screen expressing exact measures or features (e.g. architects or engineers engaged in computer-aided design).

An example of a tool that enables this is "HP SharedX" from Hewlett-Packard. It is a communication tool that lets the group members "work side-by-side, even if they are miles apart". It enables the sharing of windows of X-based applications between networked UNIX workstations or X terminals. It enables remote users to view and interact with shared windows as if they were sitting at the same workstation. It requires no change in the applications that are to be shared and new group members can be added to a session dynamically. It can be used for remote demonstrations, remote system administration, collaborative software debugging (although other methods can also be used to enable these). Because it is not a real cooperation enabling tool, but rather a conferencing administration tool, it has disadvantages too: for example, just one user can input or receive output at one time; the user must specify with whom a (each) window is to be shared; extra explicit actions are necessary for use of different mechanisms that support cooperation (e.g. tele-pointing); and finally, no multimedia communication channels are included. Examples of systems in this area are (see also Sect. 2.4) MONET (shareware), P2P (IBM), SharedX (Hewlett-Packard), ShX (shareware), WinColl (IBM), xmx (shareware) and XTV (shareware).

2.3.1.7 Computer Conferencing Software - Invisible College

Computer conferencing stands is a class of its own in that:

- It permits asynchronous (time-shifted) communication;

- It relies on the written rather than the spoken word.

It differs from electronic mail/messaging in that it provides shared files. Thus, a computer conferencing user can read, modify or otherwise contribute to a "dynamic" text file available to all participants. Multiple threads of a discussion may appear and lead to confusion, because there is usually no organised way of turn-taking. Computer conference meetings may be held over long periods of time, with participants making contributions in their own time. In addition, users are not restricted to any location (e.g. the confines of a meeting room); that is, conference material may be retrieved at home or while travelling. All correspondence may be stored as document files. In particular, it can easily be transformed into hard copy records.

It is called the group version of electronic mail. Electronic mail systems are designed for person-to-person communication; filing of messages is done by the individual. Computer conferencing systems are geared toward groups; filing of messages is by group and by topic. A typical scenario is when a group is dispersed over very large distances and they meet into a very short "time window" when they are all in their offices. They would work in an asynchronous computer conference, checking in twice per day to see what had happened since they were there last, make their own comments and leave. Drafts, working documents, graphics and models are examples of information exchanged through the conferencing system.

Computer conferencing has been technically possible since the 70s, but few organisations have taken advantage of its potential. It has been difficult to get people to get used to using it as their main method of communication. More organisational than technical problems are hampering its acceptance. In the cases where it has not worked, it has typically been introduced by a forward-thinking management information system (MIS) person who realises quickly that such capabilities have more to do with a system for organising work than with a computer system. Small teams make up the majority of users of these systems because they can easily change the way they communicate (more easily than an entire company). Examples of such systems that are text-based are Caucus (Aule-tek Inc.), CyCo (University of Nottingham), Network Telepathy (shareware) and TeamLinks (Digital). Examples of such systems that are multimedia-based are CCWS (SRI), Communique (InSoft), MediaConferencing (USWest), Rapport (AT&T Bell), Slate (BBN Systems and Technologies), and TeamSync (GlobalStream).

2.3.1.8   Information-filtering Software - Needle in a Haystack

Work group often need large amounts of information that is hard to find, gather and organise. Information filters allow people to search free-form or semi-structured information. Typically, users specify search criteria to be used by the filter. There is an "electronic mail filter" (known as Information Lens) that is intended to help users to filter their incoming mail messages.

Nevertheless, information filtering (or more simplistically - text filtering systems) are still more of a concept than a commercial reality. The biggest problem is that to be powerful enough, and thus interesting, they require extensive pre-structuring of the information by the sending user, which means behaviour changes for the users. Examples of systems that have taken this approach are Answer Garden (shareware), InVision (shareware), Notes (Lotus Corp.), ObjectLens/InformationLens (MIT), OVAL (MIT), and WinRules (Beyond Inc.).

2.3.1.9 Computer-supported Video Tele-conferences

Tele-conferencing is the use of electronic communication to enable people to meet in spite of physical separation. Tele-conferencing systems and services are the main set of technologies developed to support group work. Within this set of technologies, video-conferencing is often thought of as a new, futuristic communication mode that lies between the telephone call and the face-to-face meeting. In fact, video-conferencing has been commercially available for almost three decades. But over this time tele-conferencing has failed to become more than a revolutionary concept on the border of success.

Intuitively, it would seem that video-conferencing is the closest thing to "being there". Furthermore, there is solid justification in terms of "hard dollar" losses. These are brought about by the increasing evidence that tele-conferencing is not the communication mode that lies between the telephone call and the face-to-face meeting, and there are few examples of travel substitution directly attributable to tele-conferencing. Furthermore, it is becoming increasingly clear that the success of these technologies is much more dependent on the nature of the application for which they are introduced than on system details and features.

Rising business travel costs spurred on the idea that most business meetings could be conducted over two-way television or similar systems. However, in spite of brilliant market forecasts, with rosy demand models and attitude surveys to back them, and the appearance of great activity generated by the flurry of (face-to-face) conferences, seminars, demonstrations and articles about tele-conferencing, the base of video-conferencing systems installed in 1984 was pitifully small. A recent estimate suggests there are 210 systems in the USA, spread over some 75 companies, including telephone companies and tele-conferencing vendors.

An analysis of tele-conferencing and related literature points to two broad factors responsible for the discrepancy between video-conferencing market forecasts and current realisations. First, consider the inadequacy of needs assessment methodologies. Second, consider the questionable portrayal of video-conferencing as a direct replacement for face-to-face meetings.

The decreasing cost of bandwidth, the proliferation of satellite communication, and the emergence of cheaper, more convenient technologies and of new video-based services are often mentioned as factors that may increase the utility of a video capability. It is possible that the current explosion in office automation systems, and the resulting attitudinal changes toward high technology, may open some avenues for related technologies such as tele-conferencing. Examples of systems that have taken this approach are CAVECAT (University Toronto), GTCS (IIS Technologies), LiveBoard (Xerox PARC), Mermaid (shareware), Rapport (AT&T Bell), TeamWorkstation (NTT), and VISIT (Northern Telecom).

2.3.1.10   Conversational Structuring - Say What You Mean

Communication among group members is a critical aspect of a group's performance, eventhough little thought is usually given to how to structure this communication most effectively. One approach to computer-supported groups is to develop or select a structure for group conversations that will be closely in keeping with the task and style of the group members themselves. Structured conversations might increase both efficiency and effectiveness.

It is an unusual approach to software development. It requires building explicit forms of communication, i.e. structuring what most groups usually do in unstructured ways. The first commercial software to take a significant step forward in this field was "The Coordinator". It is known that structuring conversations is a risky business. It can be perceived as intrusive or worse. Careful thought must be given to what structures make the most sense for a given group, as well as how to introduce the structures once they have been selected. Examples are the above Coordinator (Action Technologies Inc.), InFocus and Together (Coordination Technology Inc.) and PAGES (University of Helsinki).

2.3.1.11   Computer-supported Spontaneous Interaction

It is most often said that the most important group meetings happen around coffee pots or in hallways. Electronic systems can encourage this type of interaction. A typical scenario is: it is almost midnight and Karen is about to log off. She receives a notification from the system that Helen has just logged on. After a short text message they connect over the audio channel (neither of them is interested in having the video channel at this time of the night after working for 16 hours!!!). A constructive conversation follows, the kind that would rarely happen at the office during the day with a couple of students rushing about.

Current technology allows "drop-in" encounters over electronic media. This communication is very important for groups, and it certainly occurs much more frequently than formal meetings in meeting or conference rooms. The major hurdle is the cost/bandwidth balance of the (audio and video) communication channels (see [Johansen 89]). Examples of systems that have taken this approach are CAVECAT (University of Toronto), Media Spaces,

Portholes and RAVE (Xerox EuroPARC), MEET (QMW College), and Cruise Machine (Bellcore).

2.3.1.12 Comprehensive Work Group Support: Multimedia

Work groups have many support needs, and an integrated computer system is certainly attractive. Obviously this type of support is difficult to provide, even when it is just for one type of group. The use of different interaction media or documents type can certainly increase group effectiveness.

Desktop, full-motion digital video brings a new level of collaboration and communication. It means a continuous sequence of video images integrated in the workstation or PC, and the ability to capture, archive, edit, display and transmit new horizons of information. Just as e-mail can include images and audio, it also include a sequence of images. A mail application could enable users to place and edit digitised video in a standard e-mail message. The video sequence might have been captured from a television broadcast, an in-house talk, a trade show demonstration or a synthetic scene generated by a computer. Video processing enables the user to capture video clips, then manipulate and store them. Different aspect include dropping and duplicating frames, creating special effects, synchronising audio and video, splicing clips together and so on. These capacities can be very important in the production of group authoring and editing software, information filtering software, project management software and calendar management for groups. The challenge of ease-of-use of video on the computer by groups is not so predictable. Widespread use is not likely to occur until multimedia presentations (for single user) are as easy as creating slides or displaying analogue video on a VCR.

Audio plays an important role in cooperative multimedia applications. When a representative adds a voice note to a credit record, when executives hold a video conference, listen to voice mail or have their e-mail read to them over the telephone, they all use desktop audio (perhaps integrated with other media). Audio can be used in many applications, such as voice annotation, voice conferencing, voice mail, training and presentations, text-to-speech, and so on.

A pitfall of today's integrated products is that users think that the specific functionalities they find in the integrated systems are not so powerful as the ones they would be using in stand-alone specialised systems. This represents an inevitable trade-off between the values of integration and the power within specific solutions. Also, integrated systems are likely to be expensive and are probably not compatible with the mainstream software on the market (see [Johansen 89]).

2.3.1.13   Non-human "participants" in Group Meetings

At some point computer programs should approximate their functioning and capabilities to the way humans work. This is dependent on substantial advances in Artificial Intelligence, and there are still no real examples of this. There is growing interest in having Expert Systems as a "knowledge medium", whereby people communicate through the expert system, rather than simply extracting information from it as an autonomous system. Designing systems that are though of as people or group members may be misleading, and perhaps counterproductive. Today's state-of-the-art technology in general shows that systems are a long way from personhood; care must be taken that the "non-human participant" is not misunderstood by human group members.

2.3.2   Sorting and Analysing the Approaches

We think it is now useful to try out various classifications of these different approaches. Fig. 2.5 shows the several approaches in order of increasing difficulty of realisation.

Looking through the approaches summarised in Fig. 2.5, shows that a number of different groupings are possible. The most useful method was to categorise the approaches according to one of the fundamentals of any work group: the meeting. A broad definition of "meeting" is meant here, including any form of group interaction. The approaches can then be classified in the following categories: support for face-to-face meetings, support for electronic meetings and support between meetings (Fig. 2.6 reflects this).

1	Group decision support systems
2	Project management software
3	Calendar management for groups
4	Group authoring and editing software
5	Computer-supported face-to-face meetings
6	Screen-sharing software
7	Computer conferencing software
8	Information-filtering software
9	Computer-supported video tele-conferences
10	Conversational structuring
11	Computer-supported spontaneous interaction
12	Comprehensive work group support: Multimedia
13	Non-human "participants" in group meetings

Fig. 2.5: Approaches to computer support for groups in increasing difficulty of realisation

In Fig. 2.6 we classify the approaches with reference to the support for group members during face-to-face meetings, remote meetings (also called geographically separated, mediated, electronic) or activities between meetings. Of course, some of the approaches could be classified in more than 1 of these 3 categories (e.g. approaches 12 and 14 could well fit in any of the classifications). Fig. 2.6 also suggests that most today's approaches to computer-supported groups focus on electronic meeting support and support between meetings. These approaches also tend toward the middle and upper end of a difficulty spectrum.

Classifying approaches to computer-supported groups according to the type of the software is only one possibility. Others might be classification by the type of support provided, synchrony or asynchrony of the group communication that occurs, the size of the group to be supported (here the approaches are rather directed to small groups) or the type of group to be supported.

Face-to-face meetings:

1	Group decision support systems
5	Computer-supported face-to-face meetings

Remote meetings:

4	Group authoring and editing software
6	Screen-sharing software
7	Computer conferencing software
8	Information-filtering software
9	Computer-supported video tele-conferences
13	Non-human "participants" in group meetings

Activities between meetings:

2	Project management software
3	Calendar management for groups
10	Conversational structuring
11	Computer-supported spontaneous interaction
12	Comprehensive work group support: Multimedia

Fig. 2.6: Classification of the approaches concerning the support of group members during face-to-face meetings, remote meetings or activities between meetings

2.3.3 Potentials of Computer-supported Groups and Obstacles to Their Emergence

Much has been said and will be said in the future, about the strength of computer-supported groups. The approaches above reveal the energy around the general concept of CSCW or computer support for groups. Probably, the most important factor in this is the general trend toward business teams. Teams have become the order of the day for many large companies. Organisational and cross-organisational groups are most common: project teams and task forces that have important authority and tight deadlines. These groups are searching for tools that will help them perform their jobs. In addition, a purchase by a business manager will be evaluated by different criteria than a purchase initiated by a data processing, visualisation or tele-communications manager. Although operational people typically worry about saving money, business teams often focus on ways to make money. From another point of view, the performance of business teams is more often tractable than the performance of large organisations. If a team has a clear task and a timetable, its productivity should be measurable. This measurability of effects should make business teams even more attractive to executives.

A second potential advantage for the emergence of computer support for groups is the acceptance by most businesses that computers can be used to gain competitive advantage. The penetration of personal computers and workstations is now at a point where interconnection of team members at their desks is usually practical. Many business people (as well as others) seem to have the feeling that their companies might have moved too fast from the mainframe to the personal workstation or personal computer. Users often realise that they want their machine connected to others, at least the ones that are close. Fuelling this trend is the increasing popularity of Local Area Networks (LANs) or any other kind of networks (see Sect. 2.2).

Up to now we have stated the promises and positive points of computer support for groups. But there are some obstacles to overcome. One, rather conceptual, is the name. There is no general agreement on the term used to designate this discipline. New disciplines are easier to grasp if they have easy "handles" to describe them. In this case the handles can be awkward. Here is a list of terms that mean about the same thing as, or at least overlap considerably with, "computer-support for groups":

- Computer-supported teams
- Computer-supported cooperative work
- Departmental computing
- Augmented knowledge workshops
- Group process support systems
- Teamware
- Decision conferences
- Collaborative systems
- Groupware
- Coordination technology
- Work group computing
- Interpersonal computing
- Computer assisted comm.
- Group decision support

A second obstacle is that group-oriented software is not easy to develop. Most of the problems lie in the "basic facts of the matter", rather than in the state-of-the-art technology. Computer scientists and developers usually have to interact with social and organisational psychologists, which is not always an easy interaction to accomplish.

A third aspect is that there are very few true success stories of group software products in the market. The approaches described above provide a clue to the range of experience currently existent, but little user experience is available. Furthermore, there are incentives for not exchanging success stories with other users when they do occur, because teams are often working on important tasks which are usually confidential and involve competitive advantage.

One potential reason why the value of CSCW seems obvious to researchers, but has not yet made a strong impression on industry, is the PC revolution of the 1980s. Potential group tasks such as writing and designing migrated from minis and mainframes to personal computers with little processor power and limited connectivity. As personal computer and workstation LANs evolved, software vendors concentrated their resources on developing more powerful single-user applications. At the same time, CSCW researchers have shied away from research on PC systems because of their limited power and lack of multitasking operating systems. Personal computing is beginning to meet the requirements of CSCW, but most CSCW prototypes are designed around UNIX workstations.

Another reason that industry is taking a wait and see attitude towards CSCW is the inconstant attitudes in CSCW research. One year it is concentrated on object-oriented design, the next on hypertext, and now on multimedia. This flickerness, coupled with a lack of solid empirical evidence supporting groupware, has left industry with little to grab onto. A prohibiting factor is the nature of CSCW prototypes. Cooperative editors are impressive in their interaction, but users have become accustomed to powerful word processors. Researchers have spent time perfecting multi-user features, leaving fonts and formatting to industry. The same can be said about other media. This puts industry developers and users in the position of comparing formatting and drawing features against coordination features. Colours and fonts will very often win.

In order for CSCW to have an impact in industry, researchers need to clarify the benefits of their prototypes and demonstrate that concepts that work well in simple applications can be useful in robust ones. We think that organisations with the following characteristics are, or can be expected to be, the major users of computer-supported groups:

- Companies with many decentralised project teams;

- Companies with a high penetration of personal computers, workstations and LANs;

- Companies with successful tele-conferencing systems;

- Companies with a flexible organisational structure;

- Companies with a record of early adoption of information systems innovations.

2.4   Cooperative Multimedia Editing

Cooperative multimedia editing is the process of using multimedia applications to create multimedia materials within a group. It uses a wide variety of tools, from the more familiar text editor or desktop publishing application, to tools for capturing and manipulating video images or editing audio files. Co-authors might include specialised creators of training, sales or corporate applications, such as insurance claims processing, or they might be creators of everyday business communication, such as voice-annotated e-mail. It can be done on all types of media: e.g. voice, music, still images, motion video, graphics and text. Over time, everyone involved in business communication will probably have some level of multimedia editing capability.

2.4.1   Single-user Multimedia Editing

Educators, managers, sales personnel, and training directors are among those who can use multimedia editing systems to create their own customised interactive multimedia programs.

A multimedia editing system is a software application that allows application authors to easily combine different media (graphics, text, video, audio, animation and so on) into a single multimedia document, while also providing a standard interface and a structure that makes it possible for users to make non-linear, associative interconnections between different media elements. An editing system provides an non-obstructive, intuitive, yet powerful interface that can function effectively as the user's window on the information world. The author should be able to structure the several media information in a variety of ways, from a linear "slide show" presentation to a non-linear, interactive type of presentation environment. Some of the functions that a system should include are excursion branching and launch/return functions. Excursion branching enables the user to take side trips to related topics. The user can then decide to return where he had left off or continue down to another information path. Launch/return features let the user launch other applications from inside the multimedia editing tool. They provide specific tools to create customised programs. All media that are supported by an editing system can be either imported or created using the editing system. For the purpose of importing data, the more formats (text, graphics, audio and so on) an editing system supports, the better.

Usually a multimedia editing system contains its own procedural language or offers the user direct access to such a language. This procedural language takes, in most cases, the form of a script language. One is often led to think that animation is superfluous to an editing system that provides video capacities. We think that this is not true, because in many cases good animation is just as valuable as a good video. For example, it would be difficult to videotape a chemical reaction from inside a sealed tank. However, an animation sequence of the reaction could be as descriptive as the video sequence and much safer to produce. Controlling external media is also an important feature present in editing systems. Such systems provide, in the majority of the cases, drivers for several remote-media peripherals. In putting together a multimedia system, one should not be little the advantages of other adjunct tools that add expressiveness to the multimedia projects, such as graphics software, scanners, video digitisers, audio digitisers, sample editors, video-editing software, titling software, specialised script-writing and story boarding software, general purpose software (project managers, spreadsheets, word processors, and desktop publishing programs). Examples in the marketplace are: Guide, Macromind Director Interactive, Authology Multimedia, InfoWindow, Hypercard and MediaTracks.

2.4.2 Cooperative Single-media Editing

Different approaches to the problems of cooperative editing have been taken and several prototypes have been built. Most of the cooperative single-media editors (products or research systems) work with the text or graphic media. Therefore, we divide our description of representative examples (much more exist) in three parts: text medium, raster images medium and 2D-graphics medium.

2.4.2.1 Text Medium

ICICLE: (Intelligent Code Inspection Environment in a C Language Environment) is intended to augment the efficiency of formal code inspection. It supports knowledge-based analysis of the source code, margin annotations, cooperative discussion and comments during inspection meetings. It implements social roles (moderator, reader, scribe, author and inspector), telepointing, and relaxed-WYSIWIS. It is to be used in face-to-face situations. ICICLE runs on Sun workstations with X Windows and has been developed in Bellcore (see [Brothers et al. 90]).

ShrEdit: is a multi-user text editor that allows users to edit simultaneously a text file having true concurrent access (there is just one copy of the document). The changes are reflected for all (relaxed-WYSIWIS) and there exists a position lock mechanism. It provides no user identifications (e.g. the position of the editing operations of the co-authors is not shown), although each user has their own (personalised) cursor and telepointer. The user can "park" him/herself, being then just a watcher. It has also mechanisms for session control, explicit social roles and brainstorming, and can be used for synchronous as well as asynchronous editing. It has been developed at the University of Michigan and runs at Macintosh (see [Olson et al. 90, McGuffin 92]).

SASE, SASSE and SASSSE: are developments of a group text editor. They can be used on Macintosh and assume that people communicate via telephone or another audio/video connection. They support relaxed- and strict-WYSIWIS, tele-pointing and personalised coloured text for co-author awareness. A position lock mechanism with variable graining, is inconporated. In the replicated architecture a copy of the application and the shared document reside on each co-author's computer. The application copies communicate via TPC/IP and all message traffic is routed through the central communication server which also ensures consistency. It has been developed at the University of Toronto (see [Baecker et al. 92]).

Augment: is a text processing system marketed by Tymshare for a multi-user, network environment. The user interface facilitates flexible evolution of command languages and provides optional command recognition features. Files are hierarchically structured, and textual address expressions can flexibly specify any text entity in any file. It is possible to view the files in different options: level clipping, paragraph truncation and content filtering (see [Engelbart 88]).

Grove: (GRoup Outline Viewing Editor) is a synchronous, multi-user editor for the creation and editing of textual outline documents (tree-structured documents which can be viewed at different levels of specificity). It is designed for both face-to-face and remote collaboration situations. It supplies audio channels to support informal awareness. Outline nodes can be open, closed or terminal, and parts of the document are presented to each co-author in a view that can be public, private or shared. Access mechanisms can be used to control who can see, edit or create a node. Grove was developed at MCC (see [Ellis et al. 91]).

DistEdit: is a toolkit that can be used to build cooperative editors out of traditional single-user text editors. The sense of the word "cooperative" here is limited. Almost any single-user editor can be transformed to support collaboration. It supports the use of different editors within the same editing group, so that the users do not need to get used to a new application in order to collaborate, because all the functionalities and interface mechanisms are maintained. It provides two social roles (master and observer), although only the master role has editing capacities and there can only be one master at a time. It allows explicit and implicit locking of regions. There are no multi-user interface mechanisms (see [Knister et al. 90]). DistEdit has been developed at the University of Michigan.

Quilt: is a collaborative document production system that is based on observational studies of writers. It concentrates on user communication and annotation but also provides revision suggestion, messaging and notification facilities. It combines concepts of social aspects of the writing task, hypertext, and direct-manipulation interfaces. It provides social roles (co-author, commenter, and reader) and cooperation types (shared, exclusive, and editor). It supports co-author information, several access modes, and asynchronous editing and brainstorming. The user can customise the definitions of document, annotations, social role, and access permissions (see [Fish et al. 88]). It has been developed at Bellcore.

PREP: focuses on enhancing the effectiveness of loosely coupled collaboration. The environment is intended to support the collaborative brainstorming, authoring, reviewing, commentating and editing associated with work "in preparation". It uses organisational techniques other than the usual text editors with a heavy emphasis on hypermedia techniques. It allows users to create chunks, which correspond to ideas (containing text, grids, trees, and images) and links connecting the chunks, so that the user can build networks of ideas. To support collaboration the system allows the creation of related columns of chunks. One column can form the contents of a paper and another the paper plan. Comments can be added in another column, as can annotations and notes. It supports social roles (co-author, commenter and reader), comments, several access modes, asynchronous editing and communication about plans (see [Neuwirth et al. 90]). It has been developed at Carnegie Mellon University.

2.4.2.2   Raster Images Medium

GroupSketch and XGroupSketch: GroupSketch is a minimalist multiuser sketch-pad implementing strict-WYSIWIS, synchronous access and geographically distributed editing. It supplies personalised multiple cursors and gesturing. Four action modes are supported: gesturing, drawing, typing and erasing. XGroupSketch is a re-implementation of GroupSketch running over X Windows and including more editing features, individual co-author information and relaxed-WYSIWIS. They have been developed at the University of Calgary.

Commune: is modelled after a notepad of paper, and is intended to allow geographically separated designers to share a draw surface (see [Bly et al. 90]). Each site has a horizontal monitor and transparent digitising pad with a stylus, which serves as the writing surface. This improves control/display compatibility and fine motor coordination. It explores people's ability not only to make marks simultaneously in the workspace, but also to use cursors to support gesturing.

Wscrawl: is a shared drawing tool which allows co-authors to work on a single drawing. It can be thought of as a colour paint program that runs on several user's at once. It supports strict-WYSIWIS, gesturing and personalised multiple cursors. Wscrawl has been developed at Apple Computer (see [Wilson 92]).

2.4.2.3   2D-graphics Medium

GroupDraw: is a 2D-object-oriented multi-user drawing editor implementing WYSIWIS, synchronous access and geographically distributed editing. Unlike the examples of Sect. 2.4.2.2, co-author create objects (such as lines and squares) than can then be accessed as objects (not as sets of pixels). It supports personalised multiple cursors, gesturing and private drawings. There is as little locking of objects as possible: users can grab different endpoints of the same object. It has been developed at the University of Calgary.

GroupGraphics: is a PC/LAN environment to support enterprise analysis and graphical brainstorming (see [Pendergast 92]). GroupGraphics allows editing of object-based drawings, as opposed to bitmap sketches. It provides relaxed-, or strict-WYSIWIS, personalised multiple cursors, gesturing, telepointers and object locking. It has been developed by the University of Arizona and Ventana Corporation.

SimpleDraw, NomadicDraw and ConversationBoard: all implement a shared canvas on which co-authors can manipulate objects simultaneously and allow remote use of conversational props. Several types of floor policies have been implemented, namely token-passing and locks that time out. A form of WYSIWIS is present, as well as tele-pointing and gesturing. Audio/video communication must be supported in parallel by another application. This work has been developed at Bellcore; see [Brinck et al. 92] for more information.

Ensemble: is a concurrent object-oriented graphics editor. It uses implicit locking of graphic objects, gesturing, concurrency control at the file level and multiple cursors. It has been developed at the University of Florida (see [Newman-Wolfe et al. 92]).

2.4.3   Cooperative Multimedia Editing

By cooperative editing we mean the coordinated manipulation of information by a group of authors. During the editing process the (co-)authors need to communicate their ideas, drafts and constraints (remotely or face-to-face) until a final version of the information is achieved. For the different phases of this process (discussion of ideas, editing, cross-checking) different media are required.

Cooperative multimedia editing can be defined as the set of activities in which a group of co-authors cooperate to produce a multimedia document using multimedia techniques, namely for communication. This document can contain not only text but also other media, such as raster images, 2D-graphics, audio, voice and video. The communication channels that the co-authors use to cooperate are not only written messages but also voice, video, drawings and sketches.

Examples of application uses for cooperative multimedia editing are the areas in which the documents to be produced are multimedia documents, which involve people with different backgrounds: scientific reports (more than one author), newspaper articles, project proposals (several partners), source code production (several programmers and designers), design of rendering scenes for publicity (several designers), animation scripts or several kinds of object modelling or a conference programme (conference programme committee) - see [Santos 93a].

Aspects: combines text, graphics and pixel images in a joint editor. Like in DistEdit a scheme for combining and augmenting single-user, single-medium applications was used. The user can create the documents or use the ones that have already been created by other single-medium, single-user applications. It has the advantage that the users do not need to get used to a new application in order to collaborate. It supports WYSIWIS, personalised multiple cursors (but no other forms of user identification), synchronous and asynchronous editing. The participants can be in the same room or spread around the world. It provides roles - mediator and participant, sharing modes - one user, a set of users and everyone and cooperation types - free-for-all, medium, and full mediations. There is a registration protocol. It was developed by Group Technologies (see [Biel 91]).

Slate: is a multimedia conferencing and document-preparation system. The underlying theory is that interactions, and conferences especially, focus on documents to be collaboratively viewed/edited/reviewed. This way, it concentrates on the document-related portions of the conference, assuming that other channels will be used for audio and video communication. It integrates six media in a seamless environment. It is a shared window teleconferencing tool, multimedia editor and mail system. It supports WYSIWIS, synchronous and asynchronous editing, gesturing, geographically separated groups, annotations and comments and a floor control mechanism. It was developed by BBN Systems and Technologies.

Notes: is an application development environment that can support communication, coordination and collaboration within groups or organisations. It is a radically tailorable tool and it can be used to help people schedule meetings, track progress of different projects and exchange views and information on particular topics. It only supports individual asynchronous contributions. While some features, such as electronic mail are built-in, others need to be built in by the adopting organisation: discussion spaces, customised views, shared databases, and so on. Examples of applications built on top of Notes are: Beyond Notes Connection (Beyond Inc.), ELF (EDventure Holdings Inc.), EUCOS workflow system (University of Paderborn), Lotus Chronicle (Lotus Corp.) and QuoteMaster (Planning Consultancy).

TeamWorkStation: is designed to bridge the gaps between personal computers, traditional design desktop and telecommunication. It provides distributed users with a real-time open shared workspace which every member can see, point to, and draw on simultaneously by using heterogeneous tools. The key design idea, translucent overlay of individual workspace images, consists of superimposing two or more translucent live-video images of computer screens or physical desktop surfaces. The overlay function created with this video synthesis technique allows users to combine individual workspaces, and to point to and draw on the overlaid images simultaneously. The shared screen of TeamWorkStation is a strict implementation of the WYSIWIS design principle. The combination of individual and shared screen, however, relaxes the space constrains of WYSIWIS. TeamWorkStation was developed at the NTT Human Interface Laboratories (see [Ishii et al. 91]).

2.5   Usability Study

Evaluating software for support of group work and multimedia has two components. The first component involves the usual criteria and methods applied to the evaluation of any software product. The second component addresses those issues that are unique to group work.

Usability evaluation is of importance to everyone dealing with information technology, and people are increasingly aware of its significance. Usability reflects all those aspects of a system which enable people to make use of the system effectively, efficiently and with satisfaction. It is affected by factors ranging from detailed design decisions about screen layout to the broadest organisational issues.

To be reliable and cost-effective, the process of evaluation must use suitable methods. Evaluation methods help us diagnose what is wrong with a design or identify specific factors which make the system difficult to use, so that it can be improved.

Today, no one can predict the nature of the transformations that computer technology will bring to our life, but one aspect that will be certainly affected is the way we communicate. The use of electronic mail and messages, long-distance blackboards, computer bulletin boards, instantaneously transferable data, video-conferences and cooperative synchronous editing of information is reportedly advancing "like an avalanche".

The functions and impact of computer-mediated communication and collaboration support are still poorly understood. Critical information (such as who uses it and for what purposes) is lacking, and the social significance is controversial. For instance, access to electronic communication may change the flow of information within organisations, altering status relations and organisation hierarchy. When a manager can receive electronic mail from 10 000 employees, what happens to existing controls over participation and information? When people can publish and distribute their electronic newspaper at no cost, does the distribution of power change too? When communication is rapid and purely textual, do working groups find it easier or harder to resolve conflict situations? These unanswered questions illustrate that although the technology may be impressive and capable of new wonders, little systematic research exist on its social and organisational significance. Given such conditions it seems important, even fundamental, to understand the behavioural and social process that surround cooperative multimedia interactions.

With a few pioneering exceptions, research on and analysis of computer-mediated cooperation and communication technologies evaluate the efficiency of these technologies based on their cost and technical capabilities. Representative of this orientation are discussions of how they can work in organisations such as libraries, engineering firms or offices; surveys of the introduction of computer networks in organisations; and also experimental studies comparing the effects of various communication social implications are short term. Some effects, such as increased lateral communication in an organisation or reduction in clerical staff, might develop over a long period through the actions and attitudes of many people.

In general, research on the technical capabilities of computers and systems has addressed questions about how technical, economic, or ergonomic characteristics of the technology are related to organisational efficiency and effectiveness. The synchronicity of information exchange now provided by networks might allow people to work without regard for their geographic dispersion, their schedules, time zones, access to secretaries and energy costs. If computer mail discourages chatting and off-task interaction or if people read more effectively than they listen, then managers might become more efficient for example.

Chapter 3

Modelling Cooperative Multimedia Editing

"We are not alone!"

The Hackman framework (presented in Sect. 3.1) is a descriptive model of group behaviour focusing on group tasks. There are three main notions: the group input, the group outcomes and the group coordination process connecting them and supporting the group activity. We decided to use this framework because we agree with the majority of its concepts, it is broadly accepted within the scientific community and it can be augmented to include multimedia technology, computer support and time. The Hackman framework is defined as "an organising framework which is useful in sorting out the specific relationships among (a) the initial state of a task-oriented group, (b) the group interaction process, and (c) the group's performance". However, the Hackman framework does not account for the possibility of computer-supported groups and multimedia technologies. These two aspects introduce new input factors that influence the group output. Also, the group coordination process does not deal with aspects of multimedia communication and how these can influence the group outcomes.

In Sect. 3.2, we augment this framework to include the influence of multimedia technology and computer support. To do this we examine the technology-level input factors, their influences on the group coordination effects and altogether on the group benefits. The technology-level input factors are mechanisms to be included in a prototype system in order to produce coordination effects in the groups that use it. The group coordination effects are the work habits and techniques that can be induced by the technology-level input factors. The group benefits must either directly, via improved quality or reduced time, or indirectly, via greater user satisfaction, outweigh the costs of implementation and introduction of the groupware technology.

3.1   The Hackman Framework

The Hackman framework (see [McGrath 84, Hackman 83, Hackman et al. 86])
is a descriptive model of group behaviour focusing on the group tasks. There
are three main notions: the group input, the group outcomes, and the group
coordination process that stands inbetween supporting the group activity.
We decided to use this framework because we agree with the majority of its
concepts, it can be easily and with modularity augmented to include multimedia technology concepts, and it is broadly accepted within the scientific
community. The Hackman framework is useful in sorting out the relationships among: the initial state of a task-oriented group, the group interaction
process and the group's performance effectiveness This general paradigm has
been referred in the literature, namely in [McGrath 84] and used as a reference concept for group research since it was presented. It has been developed
to combine small group research and significantly influenced the construction
of various frameworks

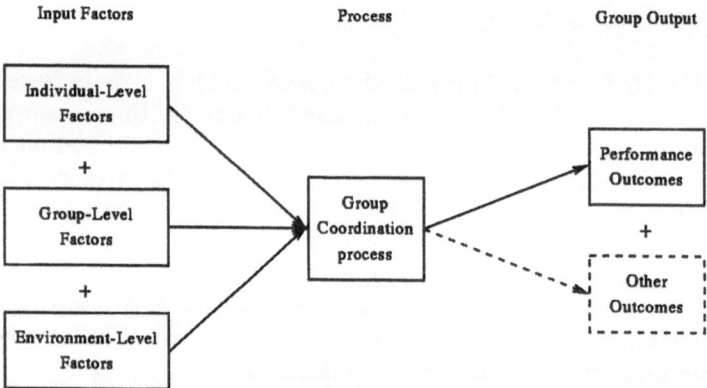

Fig. 3.1: A traditional paradigm for the analysis of the group coordination
process as a bridge between the group factors (Input) and the performance
outcomes of the group (Output)

It is depicted in Fig. 3.1 and it can be used for analysing the role of group
coordination (called "group interaction process" in [Hackman 83]) as a mediator of input-performance relationships. As used here "coordination" refers
to all observable interpersonal behaviour that happens between two points
in time for a precise definition of the notion of coordination. The state of all
system and group variables can be accessed at a given time slice, and therefore input-output relationships can be examined for periods of time ranging
from seconds to years. The longer the time period of the time slice, the
greater is the amount of group interaction existent between input time and

output time, and the more complex the analysis of the role of coordination in mediating input-output relationships becomes.

The coordination process of Fig. 3.1 recycles in a continuous way, i.e., many properties of the group and its members (e.g. group communication structures, individual attitudes) both affect the nature of the coordination and are themselves affected by that process. Such effects of the coordination process can affect the nature of subsequent coordination, leading to their further modification, and so on. The fundamental assumption of the paradigm in Fig. 3.1 is that input factors affect performance outcomes through the coordination process. Thus, if a group with some determined characteristics (e.g. high cohesion, composed of highly competent members) performs better on some task that another with other characteristics it should be possible to explain this difference in performance by examining the two coordination processes. By appropriate analysis of the coordination process it should be possible to develop a complete understanding of input-output relationships in any performance setting. Hackman even writes (see [Hackman 83]) that the input-performance relationships are always available - albeit sometimes well hidden - in the coordination process itself.

3.1.1   Three Input Factors

Individual-level factors:
- Individual capacities and skill
- Pattern of member skill
- Individual attitudes
- Personality characteristics
- Member personality

Group-level factors:
- Structure, history, cohesion
- Individual roles
- Level of cohesion
- Individual attitudes, conflicts
- Group inter-disciplinarity
- Leader attitudes

Environment-level factors:
- Group task characteristics
- Organisational constraints
- Type of organisation
- Various deadlines
- Reward structure
- Environmental stress level

There are three kinds of input factors. The ones that have to do just with the individual, the ones that are characteristic of the group, and the ones that come from the environment that surrounds the group.

3.1.2   The Group Coordination Process

The group coordination process stands in the middle serving as a bridge from the input factors to the group outcomes. Several authors have discussed the determinants and consequences of the group coordination process in the context of this framework (see [Hackman 83, Galegher et at. 90a, Bodker et al. 88, Neuwirth et al. 90, Greif 88]). There are three types of studies, namely (a) those that deal with input-process relationships; (b) those that focus on process-output relationships; and (c) those that focus on the input-process-output relationships (to complete the sequence). It has been established that several input factors of group work affect the coordination process, namely its nature and direction. Among the input factors that have been shown to affect group coordination are the nature of the task (e.g. type, difficulty, granularity), leader attitudes, member personality, group structure, group history, technology used and so on. Several analyses revealed not only "how much" relationship exists between the group coordination process and group performance, but also what specific aspects of the coordination and what specific performance measures contribute most substantially to the obtained relationship.

Group coordination process:
- Cooperation management
- Context/task oriented
- Decision making
- Intra-group interaction factors
- Allowable operations
- Conflict management
- Realisation of social roles
- Intra-group comm. factors
- Intra-group cooperation factors

3.1.3 Group Performance Outcomes

The performance outcomes form just part of the group outcomes. There are several types of group outcomes, such as the tangible output (usually a document), the time spent in the task, member satisfaction, group cohesion, and attitude change. Here we are just interested in the performance outcomes. These are the ones that have to do with the quality of the output. These performance outcomes are to be used as parameters in the measure of the "group effectiveness".

Performance outcomes:
- Performance quality
- Number of errors
- Variability of the quality
- Commitment to results
- Confidence and satisfaction
- Speed of solution
- Overall quality
- Ease and cost
- Acceptance
- Willingness to future work

3.1.4 The Three "summary variables"

As suggested by several authors in the bibliography (and expressed in Fig. 3.1), the group coordination process has a central and transitional role between the input factors and the group outputs. Exactly how such a transition role can be defined is a question for hard discussions. In attempting to answer this question, Hackman (see [Hackman 83]) suggests the use of a set of "summary variables" to study and control the performance outcomes of a group. The number of factors that can influence group output is so big that managing more than a few factors at a time, either conceptually or experimentally, is nearly impossible. Hackman tried to use "a set of variables in order to link conceptually and functionally all kinds of group inputs ... with the various kinds of group outputs". Following this, he proposed three general summary variables: (a) the effort that the group members make to accomplish the task; (b) the task performance strategies used by group members in carrying out the task; and (c) the knowledge and skills of the group members. It is proposed that if one could control these three summary variables, one would be able to affect the level of effectiveness of a group. In Fig. 3.2 we represent the connections of the three summary variables to the Hackman framework. As will be shown further in more detail, these have a strong relation with the coordination process and also offer a bridge of influences between the input factors and the outcomes of the group.

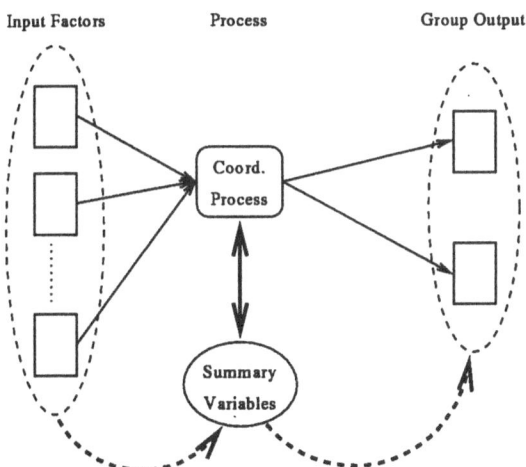

Fig. 3.2: The role of the three "summary variables" in the Hackman framework. They have a strong relation with the coordination process, are influenced by the input factors, and influence the outcomes of the group

Each of the summary variables can be affected by what happens in the group coordination process and vice versa. The interaction among group members can, for example, affect the level of effort members exert in doing the task, and can affect how well the efforts of individual group members are coordinated. On the other hand, each member's effort also has a share of influence on the quality of the coordination. Similarly, group interaction can lead to either effective or ineffective task performance strategies, and to efficient or wasteful use of the knowledge and skills of group members. Very important is the fact that the three summary variables have a different applicability factor, depending on the type of group task (some examples are given in [Hackman 83]).

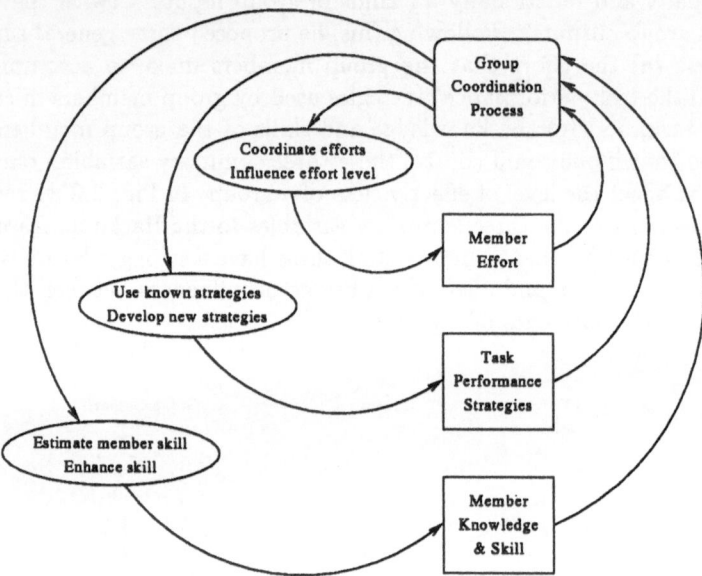

Fig. 3.3: A detailed representation of the interaction between the group coordination process and the three summary variables

We now give a brief analysis of the impact of group coordination on each of the three summary variables, i.e. how the coordination process affects group effectiveness through the summary variables.

3.1.4.1 Member Effort

How hard group members work on a task is an important determinant of group effectiveness. While many personal and situational factors can influence the level of this effort, the group coordination affects effort primarily in two ways: by affecting the coordination of the efforts on individual group members; and by affecting the level of effort group members choose to expend working on a certain group task (their task motivation). The first has to do with the fact that it is important that the members coordinate in order to minimise both the "waste" of individual efforts and the "slippage" that prevents the group from achieving its potential maximal productivity. The second effect of group coordination on the member efforts relates to the fact that relations within the group can affect how much effort an individual chooses to expend on the group task, and that this level can change over time as the characteristics of the group coordination change.

3.1.4.2   Task Performance Strategies

What specific strategies will be effective or ineffective in a given performance situation depends on the contingencies built into the task itself. However, in general terms, we can say that there are two ways in which group coordination can affect the performance strategies that a group brings to bear on its task: through implementing pre-existing strategies that are known and shared among the members; and through reformulating existing performance strategies or generating new ones. The first way has to do with the fact that when a group is given a task that belongs to a familiar class of tasks there is no need to spend time deciding how to work on the task. The second way embodies the case when either the task is unknown to the group or there is at least one member has a "new" strategy to use. Nevertheless, in this second case it was found that "planning" activities tended to be generally lower in priority that the actual task activities - even when group members were aware that it was to their advantage to engage in planning before starting the actual task.

3.1.4.3   Member Knowledge and Skill

Group coordination influences in two major ways the effectiveness with which the knowledge and skill of group members are applied to the task: estimating the possible contributions of different group members (member knowledge and skill); and creating conditions within the group which will lead to a change (presumably an increase) in the overall level of knowledge that group members have and are able to apply to the task. For some tasks the group is expected to operate at the level of its most competent member, for others at the level of the "average" member, and for others at the level of its least competent member. This requires a process of weighting the members' skills which can be provided by group coordination mechanisms. Of course, if the nature of the task is complex and subtle then the ability to predict group effectiveness (and beforehand, to estimate the suitable individual skills) simply by measuring the individual talents is reduced. The second influence of coordination is increasing the total amount of member talent available to the group for work on the task. The issue is how members can do more than merely share among themselves what they already know and gain knowledge or generate skills that previously did not exist within the group.

3.1.5   Usefulness of this Framework

The impact, shown in the last three subsections, of group cooperation on the three summary variables is summarised in the next figure.

Summary variables:	Inevitable losses:	Potential gains:
Member effort brought to bear on the task	Coordination serves as the means to coordinate and apply members effort to the task	Coordination can enhance the level of effort members expend on the task
Performance strategies used to carry out the task	Coordination serves as a vehicle for implementing pre-existing strategies shared by the members	Coordination can serve as the site to develop or reformulate strategic plans to increase their task appropriateness
Member skill and knowledge used by the group	Coordination serves as a means of assessing, weighting, and applying member talents to the task	Coordination can increase the total pool of skill available to the group

It emphasises that the roles that the group coordination can have on
the summary variables are different for each of them. This implies that, an
attempt to understand the coordination process determinants of group performance will mean examining the particular task very carefully in order to
know how operative the summary variables are. In the middle column we
represented the "inevitable" group coordination losses, and in the right column the "potential" group coordination gains of introducing or manipulating
a group coordination process between the input factors and the group outcomes. The middle column shows that there are group losses associated with
the three summary variables. The group performance therefore will depend
in part on how successful members are in finding ways to minimise these
losses. At the same time, there are (right column) group gains. At least
it is possible for members to find and implement new, task-effective ways of
coordinating which will allow them to raise the effectiveness. Sometimes, this
rise in effectiveness cannot be anticipated from knowledge about the talents
and intentions of group members prior to the start of the collective activity.

3.2   Augmenting the Input
of the Coordination Process

Referring to what has been said in Sect. 2.3.3 concerning the problems with
adoption of multimedia CSCW, especially cooperative multimedia editing,
solutions by industry, we would like to expend some effort on enumerating
and qualifying its group benefits for the users and for industry. The success
of multimedia groupware research will be determined when and if the functionality of the academic prototypes are adopted by the software industry
and users. For this to occur there must be a cost/benefit justification for
implementing groupware systems.

The Hackman framework does not account for the possibility of computer-
supported groups and multimedia technologies. These two aspects introduce
new input factors that influence the group output. Also, the group coordination process does not deal with aspects of multimedia communication and
how can these influence the group outcomes.

In this Sect. we augment the Hackman framework with one more input factor: technology. As well as the individual-level, group-level and
environment-level factors, we have now technology-level factors (TF). As an

evolution of Fig. 3.1, we have Fig. 3.4. Technology-level factors are divided in computer-supported and multimedia technology. Group coordination ef-

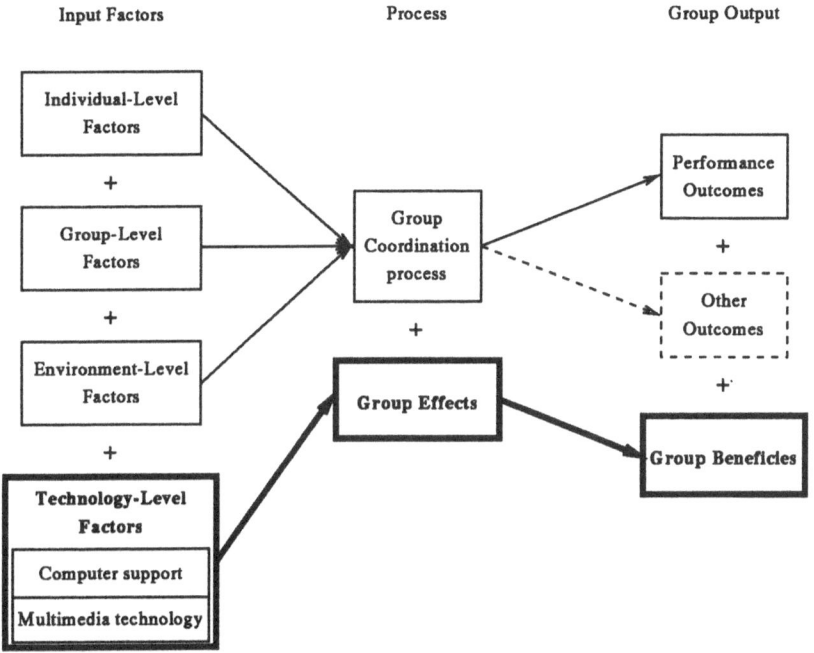

Fig. 3.4: A new paradigm for the analysis of the group coordination process, the several input factors and the performance outcomes of the group

fects (CE) are the changes in work habits and techniques. Technology-level factors are mechanisms or features that induce these habits. Mapping potential final users and industry benefits back to technology and research driven prototype systems requires this double translation. This way we state the following relationship:

Technology-level factors $\Longrightarrow$ Group coordination effects $\Longrightarrow$ Group benefits

In Sect. 4.5 we will relate the technology-level factors to the group coordination effects and to the group benefits. After explaining the advantages and disadvantages of each of the technology-level factors in Chap. 4, we can assert an evaluation schema attributing values to the several effects and benefits. Based on these we then evaluate the value of the input factors.

3.2.1 Technology-level Factors

There is a long list of technology-level input factors that can be used to produce group coordination effects. The new input factors to add are the following:

TF.1 Brainstorming: see Sect. 4.2.1;

TF.2 Registration protocols: see Sect. 4.2.2;

TF.3 Social roles: see Sect. 4.2.3;

TF.4 Multiple-cursors, tele-pointing and gesturing: the primary effect these three mechanisms have on cooperative editing is coordination of co-authors (see Sect. 4.1.1);

TF.5 WYSIWIS and synchronous update: the Strict-WYSIWIS mode increases coordination and enables such tasks as group reviews of a document and distributed presentations. Relaxed-WYSIWIS should increase the level of parallel activity and allow increased access to information. A drawback is that the co-authors are no longer (so) aware of where the others are working, therefore coordination and consistency of work can be reduced (see Sect. 4.1.2);

TF.6 Concurrent data access: is a necessary partner of the WYSIWIS and synchronous updates mechanisms. By itself it enables an increase in parallel activity, provides greater access to information and helps to promote consistency of work. Coupled with WYSIWIS and synchronous updates, it also aids in coordination of work, increases participation and enables continuous validation;

TF.7 Access techniques: it can limit the amount of parallel activity when the co-author has to request and free the resources. Automatic locking with fine granularity (Position Lock) increases data consistency and reduces integration (see Sect. 4.1.3);

TF.8 Private annotations and public comments: see Sect. 4.2.4;

TF.9 Co-author information and awareness: see Sect. 4.2.5;

TF.10 Support for latecomers: see Sect. 4.2.6;

TF.11 Structured data: the process of turning ideas and concepts into documents requires co-authors to collect integrate sequence and store data. To do this, co-authors maintain a complex mental model of the data and the structure. This is fine for individual work, but a hindrance in group editing. Adding structure and shared access to the data via multi-user hypertext systems is one solution that increases the consistency and reduces integration efforts;

TF.12 Structured tasks: for some work it is appropriate to implement a structured methodology to guide the work, e.g. group decision support. The effect of this type of strategies is to increase coordination;

TF.13 Multimedia editing: the presence of multimedia data to include in the documents can increase distributed work, information access and coordination (see Sect. 4.3);

TF.14 Multimedia communication: the addition of multimedia communication channels to the editing tools can increase tele-presence and co-presence, which in turn increases coordination, distributed work and synergy (see Sect. 4.4);

TF.15 High feedback speed and simplicity: usually enable rapid and unobtrusive construction of shared spaces and quick diffusion of ideas. Features are easier to understand, take less time to learn and thus are more user-friendly;

TF.16 Complex and high-quality features: usually enable the production of accurate, ready-to-use, high quality documents. Are more difficult to learn and more complex to use, although once learned, make the situations they were designed for easier.

TF.17 Possibility of use in any of the combinations of the Johansen matrix (see Fig. 2.2): enable the co-authors to work at any time and in any place in the documents independently of the other co-authors' work schedule.

3.2.2   Group Coordination Effects

There are several work habits and techniques that can be influenced by the technology-level factors:

CE.1 Increase in the level of parallel activity: this effect is most noticeable for editing tools which automate aspects of face-to-face meetings. The increase in parallel activity for applications which are distributed in nature, such as editing, is therefore of importance.

CE.2 Greater participation by co-authors: also most noticeable for tools which automate aspects of face-to-face meetings. Tools which allow concurrent use and that provide mechanisms which promote contributions (e.g. anonymity) encourage silent co-authors to participate;

CE.3 Fewer integration steps: this applies mainly to editing tools that use a shared workspace. Tools that require co-authors to work individually, then periodically merge their work can actually add integration steps;

CE.4 Distributed work: if the editing tool is used in a wide area fashion it will save travel time. In a local setting, distributed features enable work to be carried out at the desk of each co-author, removing the need for specialised electronic meeting rooms;

CE.5 Synergy among workers: synergy is the increase in effectiveness which comes about when people work in groups rather than individually; cooperative editing applications can either enhance this effect by providing mechanisms to allow the free flow of ideas, work and communication, or inhibit synergy by creating artificial boundaries, rules or protocols;

CE.6 Greater consistency of work: consistency in cooperative work involves such things as using the same diagramming conventions or fonts, writing from the same perspective (first person, third person, etc.), and nomenclature. Some aspects can be enforced by the software, but other consistency gains are a result of better communication and access to work in progress;

CE.7 Continuous validation of contributions by co-authors: concurrent access to data and synchronous updates enable the entire team to access and review the work as it progresses. This eliminates the need for periodic review sessions and reduces the number of "surprises" which can result from people working autonomously on separate parts of a document;

CE.8 Increased access to information: this is accomplished by both allowing concurrent access to data and providing better methods to access the data;

CE.9 Greater coordination of group work: coordination of the editing work implies both the use of the shared workspace, i.e. spatial arrangement, and the coordination of actions. The latter can be achieved by enforcement of co-author behaviour rules (e.g. social roles), and/or can be supported by social protocols established between the users via the communication channels.

3.2.3 Group Benefits

The group benefits must either directly, via improved quality or reduced time, or indirectly, via greater user satisfaction, outweigh the costs of implementation and introduction. This way, we have the following group benefits:

- Reduced work and travel time;

- Increased output quality;

- Greater user satisfaction and efficiency;

- Retention of other known advantages of face-to-face situations and/or single-user systems. Examples are the social context, spontaneity, socialisation possibilities, use of high developed and accepted single-user software functionalities and use of previously learned know-how relating to single-user systems.

Chapter 4

Concept of the Prototype Tool

> *"We are living in a small, unique and precious harbour of life; our competence at cooperating is ultimately our salvation."*

Let me begin this chapter with a practical example observed during a recent stay in a hospital (Städtische Kliniken Darmstadt) due to an accident. It was interesting how much coordination and negotiation took place among nurses over their clipboards using documents and other information about the patients. In spite of the regular daily meetings to clarify the state of the patients, they carried on informal interactions in the hallway. Introducing information processing to this hospital situation, the first bad idea might be to make the documents only available on a workstation. That would completely ignore the informal conversations and interactions of the nurses. The nurses might probably cope with this poorly designed computer system. However, to be most helpful, the technology of record keeping and conversation should be as familiar and easy to use as the clipboard, paper and pen. The lesson to be learned is that special attention must be paid not only to technological factors, but also to human factors when designing groupware systems.

In this chapter we propose and defend the underlying design requirements for a cooperative multimedia editing prototype tool. These surely apply to a wider range of tools. There is a number of different approaches to the development of cooperative multimedia editing systems. One way is to modify existing single-user, single-medium systems. This has the advantage of producing quick results (being cheaper); it requires less forethought, and the users may already be familiar with the systems. However, as the tools must be accepted by all the group members, it is difficult to find a set of single-user tools that is broadly accepted. Also, these solutions are less flexible and less powerful since collaboration varieties depend on user ingenuity and are more dependent on extra-system technologies. We adopted a different approach, namely we conceptualised and developed a tool from scratch to coherently integrate the principles exposed in this chapter. The advantages of this approach are that it is more flexible, it enables wider varieties of cooperation and it is less dependent on extra-system technologies. The disadvantages are that it is costly, requires more forethought and more experience and the solutions are often application-specific. We developed the multimedia editors and the communication facilities to maximise user commodity and group support. We adopted a problem-oriented rather than a task-oriented approach, i.e. instead of having clear prescriptions assuming one best way of performing a certain kind of task, we have a flexible array of utilities, which are open and can be used according to the characteristics of the problem to be solved or the goal to be achieved.

In Sect. 4.1 we show how multi-user interfaces differ from single-user interfaces, namely in that they depict group activity and are controlled by multiple users rather than a single-user. An example of a basic problem is how to manage complexity: multiple users can produce a higher level of activity and a greater degree of parallelism than single users, and the interface must support this complex behaviour. Other important questions that can be mentioned are what kind of single-user interface mechanisms, techniques and concepts are useful for constructing multi-user interfaces. An example of this is whether a scrollbar is useful when it can be manipulated by more than one person, or is simply too distracting.

In Sect. 4.3 we consider the multimedia editing capabilities a prototype tool should have. The prototype tool is to be used in informal situations with the emphasis on rapid and unobtrusive construction of common documents, rather than the production of high-quality ready documents. This was because of the limited hardware we had available (e.g. mouse) and because the emphasis is on the multimedia and cooperation features rather than on the (graphic) quality of the output. If a group of co-authors requires a tool to produce a high quality logo or advertisement video, they should use prototype tool for the conceptualisation and draft phases and then specialised tools for the final product.

In Sect. 4.4 we examine the ideas behind the use of multimedia communication within a work group. Recent research has been concerned with the effectiveness of information exchange in work groups that use computer technology to meet supported by non-multimedia and multimedia communication channels. Multimedia communication has been portrayed in vendor publications as a technological marvel for increasing group information and productivity. We investigate whether this idea is correct. Also important is to investigate whether a potential increase in media types, combination or bandwidth results in an overall increase in communication (possibly implying information overflow).

In the last Sect. we present an evaluation of the technology-level input factors based on a quantitative value of each of the group coordination effects. The technology-level input factors roughly correspond to the features and mechanisms conceptualised in Sects. 4.1 to 4.4. The evaluation represents the group benefits that each technology-level input factor can bring to an application.

4.1 Multi-user Interface

Multi-user interfaces differ from single-user interfaces in that they depict group activity and are controlled by multiple users rather than a single-user. Multi-user interfaces introduce design problems not presented by single-user interfaces. An example of a basic problem is how to manage complexity: multiple users can produce a higher level of activity and a greater degree of parallelism than single users, and the interface must support this complex behaviour. Other important questions are what kind of single-user interface mechanisms, techniques and concepts are useful for constructing multi-user interfaces. An example of this is whether a scrollbar is useful when it can be manipulated by more than one person, or is simply too distracting.

A good multi-user interface should depict overall group activity and at the same time not be too distracting. For example, when a user creates, scrolls or opens a group window, or modifies an object (of any medium) another person is editing, other users can be distracted. This points up a fundamental difference between single-user interfaces and multi-user interfaces. With single-user interfaces, users usually have the mental context to interpret any display changes that result from their actions. As a result, the sudden disappearance of text at the touch of a button is acceptable; in fact, much effort goes into increasing the system's responsiveness. By contrast, with multi-user interfaces, users are generally not as aware of others' contexts and can less easily interpret sudden display changes resulting from others' actions. What is usually needed are ways of providing contextual clues to the group's activity. A simple solution is for participants to announce their intentions prior to taking action - suitable in some situations but often burdensome. Another alternative is to use animation to depict smoothly changing group activity (see also Sect. 4.1.2) or provide enough explicit questions eliciting information about the group members engaged in activity. Any solution to these sets of problems must take into account the equally important needs for speed, continuity and user friendliness: the system responsiveness to the user making changes must not be sacrificed for the smooth, continuous notification of the others.

Multi-user interfaces must match a group's usage patterns. As an example, single-user text editors often rely on simple interfaces: characters appear and disappear as they are inserted and deleted. Multi-user text editors must contend with a diversity of usage patterns. The text can be generated as inde-

pendent, reflective, consensus, and partitioned entries and, therefore, requires
much richer interface mechanisms. The same happens for other media. An
example of a solution already tried is given in [Ellis et al. 91]. It is a model
to be used for text editing by a group of co-authors. First, the text is aged
so that recently entered text appears in bright blue and then changes gradually to black. Second, while text modifications (insertions and deletions) are
immediately visible to the person who initiates them, they are indicated on
other users' displays by the appearances of clouds over the original text. The
position and size of a cloud indicates the approximate location and extent of
the modification. Some time after a user has stopped typing, the clouds on
his or her display disappear and the new text is displayed, first in blue and
gradually changing to black. The rationale for this interface is that an active
user is only marginally interested in others' changes, which should therefore
be indicated subtly and not be disruptive. Although attractive, this approach
is very expensive in terms of both computation and network capacity. Another approach is, for example, to define several access techniques, which we
deal with below.

Screen space is a limited resource in single-user applications, but it is even
more of a problem with multi-user interfaces, in which each user can create
windows that appear on other users' screens. One approach aimed at avoiding
window proliferation is to aggregate windows in functional sets (rooms), each
of which corresponds to a particular task. Participants can than move from
one set to the other. When a set is entered, the windows associated with
that room are opened. Because we are taking a problem-oriented approach
rather than a task-oriented one we will not follow an approach of this kind.
A second approach is to let the users bear the burden of maintaining window
order.

4.1.1   Multiple-cursors, Tele-pointing and Gesturing

Systems tend to be weak on showing who is doing what. Thus, each person should be given a sense as to where the others are working and what
on, whether it is in a distant but related or unrelated part or nearby (see
[Olson et al. 90]). This can be achieved in several ways, e.g. multiple/cursors,
tele-pointing and gesturing.

Multiple-cursors are used for gesturing support[1] and tele-presence awareness. Hand gestures play a prominent role in all face-to-face activities (35%
of all actions) and it would be a major oversight to disable them when people
use computer support to meet (see Fig. 4.1 and 4.4). A multiple-cursor, in
order to be personalised, should be unique, identifying the person it belongs
to (see Fig. 4.1 and 5.2). They should always maintain their relative position
on every editing surface so that they retain their meaning and relation to the

---

[1]a)the use of body motions as a means of expression; b) a movement of a body that
expresses or emphasises an idea, sentiment, or attitude. Tele-pointing, multi-cursors and
WYSIWIS are examples of mechanisms that support gesturing

work objects (the same should happen with the tele-pointers). This synchronisation is very useful to enable the co-authors to talk and write over the communication channels about the work objects they are editing or pointing to. Gesturing is something that is often done in the context of a face-to-face conversation. Also, people often use sketching in order to gesture. Gestures are a prominent action, are typically made in relation to objects on the work surface, are often accompanied by verbal explanations and must be seen if they are to be useful. While people can execute their tasks without gesturing, much of the conversation (using the multimedia media-channels), when gesturing is not supported, is used to substitute gesturing: "I am changing the second line of the first paragraph ... can you see this comma ... I think I am going to delete it". This is cumbersome and can diminish the performance of the group and the satisfaction of the co-authors.

Fig. 4.1: An example of multi-"cursors" in a face-to-face situation

In conventional drawing and writing by small groups the participants frequently gesture over the drawing surface: to represent ideas, to signal turn-taking, to focus the attention of the group, to reference objects on the surface, etc.). One way of supporting gesturing is to provide for multiple-cursors to appear on the screen (one belonging to each participant), and several usability studies confirm the ubiquity of gesturing. We believe that gesturing can improve communication quality and participant awareness and should be provided by the prototype tool.

Physical gestures can be conveyed via multiple-cursors, tele-pointers and in synchronisation with the multimedia communication channels (see Sect. 4.4). Since gestures must be seen in order to convey information, all personalised cursors in a work surface must always be visible to all.

Even when co-authors' have totally synchronised views, it can be useful to have some means of directing the attention of the group members to some

particular location within the display (see [Olson et al. 90] and Fig. 4.2).
A special pointer/cursor should be implemented differentiating from all the
cursors of other co-authors and from each one's own cursor. Tele-pointers
widen the bandwidth of communication between co-authors by conveying
information without creating further work for them.

Fig. 4.2: An example of (tele-)pointing in a face-to-face situation

A tele-pointer is a special cursor that appears on more than one display
and that can be controlled by one co-author at a time. When it is moved
on one display, it is moved on every display. During the cooperative editing
session, each co-author can manipulate his own tele-pointer by moving the
mouse device. It is useful to be able to direct the attention of the other co-
authors to a particular location within the display (as happens in face-to-face
meetings, when a participant raises his or her voice, explicitly attracting the
attention of the others to a point or explaining it). Tele-pointers should be
unique, each identifying the person it belongs to by name. The tele-pointers
are made prominent by their larger than normal size and by the name (see
two examples in Fig. 5.3). The tele-pointer has to be "picked" in order to be
used and then "released". It is important to notice that tele-pointers can be
used simultaneously for drawing, writing or any other kind of editing activity.
It is a parallel activity that does not take any freedom from the co-author.
Not all tele-pointers will be visible in every participant's shared window.
This is to prevent a co-author from using it too much and thus annoying
the others. Another reason is that tele-pointers can convey irrelevant or
distracting information or otherwise just get in the way; it should therefore
be possible to turn it off. Each co-author should be able to express to whom
the tele-pointer can be addressed and who is initiating tele-pointing.

4.1.2   What You See Is What I See

What You See Is What I See is a standard concept by the CSCW community. Since Stefik first presented this technique several papers, systems and studies have proved its usefulness (see [Olson et al. 90, Galegher et at. 90a]). The main forms are Strict-WYSIWIS and Relaxed-WYSIWIS, although there is a range of modalities between these extremes.

WYSIWIS recognises the importance of being able to see what work the others have done and what work is in progress: to "see where their hands are". With WYSIWIS in systems that allow concurrent or simultaneous editing, not only are the editing locations of the group members shown, but also the changes are shown immediately after they are performed in the remote workplaces. If the edit locations are shown using personalised cursors then even an identification of the co-authors who are editing at a certain position is possible. As participants track other's cursors and editing actions, they naturally associate the actions at the editing surface with the people who are executing those actions, promoting a close sense of proximity.

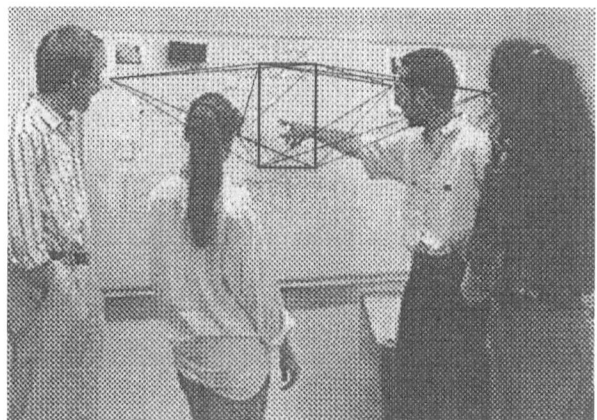

Fig. 4.3: A face-to-face meeting where Strict-WYSIWIS is being used by all participants. They are all looking to the same location of the white board

In Strict-WYSIWIS, also known as "synchronised view", all co-authors share the same view as if they were looking at the same display (see Fig. 4.3). The Strict-WYSIWIS view-sharing paradigm is the earliest and most obvious paradigm for view sharing. Strict-WYSIWIS supports a chalk-board type of interaction, where every co-author sees the same view of the shared objects. Two main advantages are that the co-authors are always aware (without any further effort) of what the others are doing and that it realises the metaphor of a piece of paper being worked upon by a group of people in a meeting. Disadvantages appear when displays with different sizes and resolutions are used and the windows are placed in different parts of the display. What is very important is that when any edit action is made at a place in the local window (independently of all the above factors), the same logical place is affected at the remote workplaces. Also, Strict-WYSIWIS makes the work somehow unnatural because, for example, someone can scroll the window where a co-author is just editing, making its insertion position change position or even disappear (the same happens with overlapping or moving windows). Another major shortcoming of this method is the lack of privacy for the co-author, as it excludes any private work space. In addition, many problems present themselves in accommodating user control of one's view of the shared data (see [Stefik 86, Stefik et al. 87]). Except for closely coupled group work, this technique is too restrictive. Thus, a number of mechanisms have been devised to relax the Strict-WYSIWIS paradigm.

Fig. 4.4: A face-to-face meeting where Relaxed-WYSIWIS is being used by the participants. They can all see a part of the common location of the white board, allowing different viewing perspectives, but they also see "private" locations outside of the common location

The most obvious relaxation consists in having independent views for each co-author (see Fig. 4.4). In Relaxed-WYSIWIS the co-authors can see the same working area if they want to or if they are working in the same region: it allows independent viewing perspectives and private work spaces. This also means that co-authors share the document, not the views.

Between these two extremes there are several other possibilities. One is Echo-WYSIWIS, in which the congruence of the displays when a co-author is carrying out a command that requires feedback (such as dragging an object) is relaxed. Instead of a display in the other co-authors' views of the exact feedback provided to the co-author issuing the command, a simplified echo is provided. When a co-author starts a command, the others only see an icon depicting the command being carried out. This tells them that something is going to happen. When the command is finished, the icon disappears and an animation shows the result of the command (or just the final result is shown).

As said before, the congruence of the document implies that when a co-author issues a command in Strict-WYSIWIS mode, the modification is immediately visible to the others. This might be disturbing if the co-authors work in a loosely coupled way. In another situation, a co-author unfamiliar with the system might not want to reveal his or her clumsiness to the group. This advocates relaxation of the congruence of the document in a way that is called Time-Relaxed-WYSIWIS, in which the modifications to the document are not visible to the others. The co-authors then, at the end of the modification, have to accept or abort it explicitly. The main drawback of this mode is the increased probability of conflicts, since all users do not work on the same version of the document.

4.1.3 Access Techniques

Also referred to as "floor control policies", or "turn-taking mechanisms", access techniques provide a way to mediate access to shared work items (text, 2D-graphic primitives, video frames and so on). Greenberg advises (see [Greenberg 91a]) that systems should "support a broad range of floor control policies" to suit co-author needs.

Systems differ in the strategy in which conflicts are eliminated, minimised or resolved. This strategy can be important in many situations, such as shared screens (of any medium) allowing only serial interaction, systems following strict interaction models (such as a teacher controlling which student can access the work surface) or systems with completely free interaction possibilities (from the co-author point of view, although for the underlying system the interactions must be serialised). At times, for maintaining consistency or ensuring that the best qualified person carries out a certain task, it can be useful for one co-author to have exclusive access to part or all of the document (in opposition to free-for-all access).

There are systems that offer no shared views, but rather lock out a co-author from an area that another co-author is working on. Other systems have locking of an insertion position. This means that a co-author cannot position its cursor on the same insertion position of another co-author, or backspace or sweep/select over another co-author's insertion position. This must be made clear to each co-author by a suitable user interface. Also, whichever mechanism is used, the (potential) conflicts must be resolved centrally by a server process that must manage the accesses of all co-authors.

4.2 Support for Cooperation

4.2.1 Brainstorming Support

Chalkboards provide a shared and focused memory for a meeting, allowing flexible placement of text and Figs., which complements our human capabilities for manipulating spatial memories. However, space is limited and items disappear when that space is needed for some more sketching (rearranging items is inconvenient when they must be manually drawn and then erased). This is the paradigm behind a brainstorming area to be supported by a cooperative editing tool.

Idea generation is a critical component of many group activities. Everyone's intuition suggests that to generate many ideas one ought to convene a group of people and brainstorm. However, thirty years of research on brainstorming (mainly without computer support) have led to a very clear and surprising outcome: for a given set of individuals, one can get both more ideas and more high-quality ideas by having each work alone and all then pool their ideas (also called nominal groups) than by having all work together as an interacting group (see [Nunamaker et al. 91]). Amongst the most commonly discussed reasons for this are:

- Evaluation apprehension: working in a group makes one's contributions visible to others, and despite the usual brainstorming instructions not to evaluate others' ideas, the members of a group can still be reticent about contributing their ideas;

- Free riding: individual members of a group might not expend the effort since others are contributing with ideas;

- Linear air time: when only one person can speak at a time, there is limited time for each individual to contribute;

- Production blocking: because of limited air time, individuals often have to hold onto their contributions until they get a change to contribute them, and as a result they might forget them or decide not to offer them. In either case the act of holding onto them will prevent them from thinking of other ideas;

- Cognitive inertia: anyone moment only one line of ideas is being generated, since they are reported serially. Groups will therefore tend to pursue fewer different kinds of ideas.

In general, while all of these factors might play some role, it looks as if production blocking (and its associated factor, air time) is the dominant reason for the reduced productivity of real interacting groups relative to nominal ones.

Given the key role of production blocking, one obvious strategy to solve the problem is to allow interacting groups to report their ideas in parallel.

A way of introducing parallelism is to allow brainstorming groups to use a computer-based tool that enables simultaneous entry of ideas yet still allows sharing of ideas among the group members. The tool should allow the entering of ideas in graphical and textual form. It show be simple to use and not "get in the way" of the members. It should resemble as closely as possible a single-user tool that a member would use individually in a nominal group. It should be possible for the whole group not to be compelled to brainstorm at the same time (one could stay out of the process if he or she did not want to brainstorm).

4.2.2   Registration Protocol

Registration, also called "login", is the process of entering an editing session. The control of who is allowed to join an editing session is an important factor, which brings up the notion of group membership. To participate in a session a participant should know at least the name of the group and its password. This increases the probability that the person who wants to participate in the editing session is informed about what is being to be worked upon, who will participate, and so on. New co-authors should be "allowed" or "not allowed" to participate in a session by a privileged co-author who is already in the session. Sometimes spontaneous participation is desired (see [Kraut et al. 88]), while other situations require a central facilitator to handle the registration (see [Nunamaker et al. 91]). The prototype tool should support a flexible mechanism to filter the participation, but without unnecessarily complicating the registration protocol. Moreover, a co-author should be able to join and leave a session at any time.

It should be possible for each co-author to give additional personal information (more than a name and an identification number) during the registration process. This information can than be distributed to the others in the session to help the group awareness. Each editing session has one editing technique (see Sect. 4.1.3). The co-author should choose one and come to an agreement with the others about it. Also, it should be possible for the co-author to choose the social role, the personalised cursor and all other data directly related to the person. (see Sect. 4.2.3 and 4.1.1). During the registration protocol, and before being accepted in the editing session, the co-author should be aware of which members of the group are currently already in the session.

4.2.3   Group Members' Social Roles

A known fact of collaboration theory and practice is that only rarely is a group composed of equally qualified people, people with equal rights inside the group, or even people who know each other. One way of dealing with this is to enforce the definition of a hierarchy of co-authors, defining the different levels' rights and duties. Some researchers believe that groupware should impose a social model of interaction on the group. This is an explicit attempt, based on management theory, to provide methods for keeping the group to the task, enforcing roles and commitments and making the group more efficient and productive. Another solution is to enable the group to define the granularity of the hierarchy, the rights and duties and so on.

There is certainly controversy between those who believe that social rules and protocols should be defined only by the group members, by the software (see [Nunamaker et al. 91, Santos 93d]) or something inbetween (see [Greenberg 91a]). Although more flexible, the first method is more complex to use properly and to understand. We adopted the second method by defining a set of social roles. This reduces the coordination problems by specifying *proper behaviours* (responsibilities, permissible actions, restrictions, patterns of interaction) of the group members.

Effective collaboration has some tacitly held rules that enforce the existence of roles in a group. There are multiple roles, such as inventing, criticising, brainstorming, reformulating, scribing, summarising and so on. People switch roles during the group's existence and even during a meeting. This switching follows certain rules such as the rhythm or momentum. For example, in an effective face-to-face collaboration situation one group member will hold back and not interrupt a second members who is generating a stream of related ideas. This way, the set of social roles to support in the prototype tool must cover most (or all) of the possible roles during an editing session and be flexible enough.

It is an accepted fact that both face-to-face and geographically distributed meetings must have a designated chairman or leader. The primary role of the leader of a face-to-face meeting, as well as of a geographically distributed meeting (Chairperson), is to ensure the development and maintenance of favourable conditions for group performance. This includes monitoring the group for conditions that detract from performance, taking action to clarify directions and agendas, strengthening group decision, moderating and/or removing organisational barriers, facilitating group processes, and ensuring adequate resources. The Chairperson role moves between an internal, group-focused role and an external boundary management role. To be effective, a Chairperson must understand both group dynamics and the criteria for effective group performance. Also, early warning signals of group problems must be detected. Studies (see [Beck et al. 93]) reveal that group leadership can be attributed to a self-appointed leader or facilitator, to an agreed leader/facilitator/project manager, or to "no-one". This suggests that a system designer would be unjustified in assuming the presence of an agreed "leader". Also, the extent to which responsibilities were clearly divided between co-authors appeared to vary, with some evidence that it was more common for there to be overlapping areas of responsibility than not.

In editing sessions, it is clear that someone must do the editing work itself. This way the Author role is adequate to support the kind of participants that do not have a leading role in the meeting but rather process and produce the documents. This is the most used role.

It should be possible to accommodate people who want to observe the group process and perhaps, at most, comment on the group actions or on the documents being produced. This is the purpose of the Commenter role. Reviews, people who will evaluate the group or the documents, expert advisers, etc. are the functionalities supported by this role.

There must be support for "strangers", i.e. people that formally do not belong to the group but are, in some way, interested in or connected with the final product. They must be able to read the documents being processed but maintained as much as possible outside the cooperation process, so as not to disturb the participants. This role should be called Reader.

4.2.4   Private Annotations and Public Comments

Researchers at Xerox PARC studied the use of conventional drawing and writing surfaces by small groups and noted many instances of annotations made to existing drawings, serving both as gestures (e.g. underlining text while saying "this one here") and as meta-level notes. A way of annotating a thought (privately or publicly) verbally, textual or graphically is useful in many situations and should be supported. Contributors (co-authors) such as reviewers or editors of a document often record their suggestions as marginal annotations or comments.

In non-computer-supported meetings, participants frequently make comments on what the others say or write, as well as private notes of ideas to be raised afterwards. To support these two important activities co-authors can create and manipulate private annotations.

Most group editors are based on a model of access that is fully public and sharable. But many group editors have explored a variety of different mechanisms for mixing public and private work. Total privacy is achieved when some aspect of the work is available only to one person. This way, the tool should enable the creation and manipulation of annotations private to each co-author. Annotations should include the possibility of expressing ideas in more than one medium and should refer to an arbitrary spot in the document (independently of the medium).

In non-computer-supported meetings, participants frequently make comments on what the others say or write. To support these important activities co-authors can create and manipulate public comments. The same recommendations as for private annotations apply also for public comments. Additionally, a mechanism should be implemented to ensure that the comments are distributed to all co-authors in the meeting as soon as they are created.

4.2.5   Co-author Information and Awareness

Several studies of collaborative writing highlight the extent to which information sharing, knowledge of group and individual activity and coordination are central to successful collaboration (see [Galegher et at. 90a, Beck et al. 93]). These factors were also concerns in the design of our prototype tool. Information relating to these factors contributes to what is usually referred as co-author information or awareness. In these terms, awareness is an *understanding of the activities of others*, which provides *context for our own activity*. This context is used to ensure that individual activities are relevant to the group activity as a whole, and to evaluate individual actions with respect to group goals and progress.

It is important to recognise that the context within which group members collaborate is comprised of both

- The object of the collaboration (independently of the medium);

- The way in which the object is produced (independently of the medium).

We must therefore consider as context not only the content of the individual contributions, but also their character: their significance with respect to the whole group and its goals. It only by providing awareness of both aspects of group members' work that a tool would enable each individual to make sense of others' activities and tailor their own work accordingly. Systems described in the literature (see Sect. 2.4) take various approaches to this problem. There is a difference between mechanisms in which:

- The information is *passively collected, distributed* and presented in the same shared work space as the object information (editing windows);

- The information is *explicitly generated*, directed and separated from the shared work object. These are frequently restricted to synchronous systems (all members are virtually co-present and working at the same time in the same place).

Awareness of the first type is provided by the features referred to in Sects. 4.1.1, 4.1.2, 4.2.3, and 4.4 (multiple-cursors, tele-pointing, gesturing, social roles, multimedia communication channels and WYSIWIS). Multiple-cursors, tele-pointing, gesturing and WYSIWIS can help awareness because they give information, for example, about what and where the other co-authors are editing. Social roles describe an individual's relationship to the shared work objects and to other participants, and it is typically connected to a set of operations that can be performed (duties and rights). For example, an "author" role might be associated with open and save operations and a "reviewer" role might be associated with limited read and annotate (other examples are given in Sects. 4.2.3 and 5.2.3). Multimedia communication channels can help a co-author not to feel alone at his or her workplace.

Above all, a co-author can make comments to other co-authors or ask them questions in a quick and simple way, so that the feeling of being in a group (in which members can be seen and addressed) is closer to that in face-to-face situations. Awareness of the second aspect is provided by the individual and global information features.

Awareness explicitly generated (of the second type) is provided by two features, namely "Individual information" and "Global information".

A question that is usually posed is the identification of the co-authors currently participating in a editing meeting. If the editor is being used in a face-to-face situation, this information can be provided in part from the natural visual and verbal links. But even then, it can often be useful to know information related to the use of the system that is not seen or heard from the other co-authors. An example of this is to know who is currently logged into the session or is using a certain chapter. This information can be provided in a variety of ways, for example: co-author name, co-author personalised cursor, media currently used, co-author social role and co-author photo.

To get information about another co-author in isolation may not be enough. Co-authors' interactions and other aspects of the group dynamics should also be available. Examples are the kind of communication channels that is being used by the co-author at a certain moment, who is tele-pointing to whom and so on.

4.2.6 Support for Latecomers

A consequence of spontaneous and free editing sessions is that not all co-authors will join the editing sessions. Therefore, there must be a mechanism for co-authors who miss a session to get updates on the work done by others. This way, the work (files edited and system state variables) should be saved during and at the end of a session. At the beginning of a new session it should be possible to "load" the work in order to catch up where it had been left off.

Another aspect of the support for latecomers is the fact that not all co-authors are available at the same time to begin a session. As in a traditional meeting, it can be scheduled for 11:00 a.m. and the co-authors will arrive probably between 10:55 a.m. and 11:05 a.m. (or maybe even later). This means that a strategy must be supported to assist any participant that arrives later in "getting up to speed". This may involve sending the current state of the session to the latecomer, providing summary information about how the session has progressed over its lifetime and notifying the others that a new participant has arrived.

4.3   Multimedia Editing

An important trade-off involved in designing editing functionalities is the level
of functionality. With fewer functionalities, there is less for the co-authors
to learn and fewer decisions to make. But each new capability can, once
learned, make the situations it was designed for easier. If the tool takes too
much time to learn, it either will not be used or will disrupt the cooperation.

The prototype system to be built must support basic edit functionalities for each of the media supported. It is also desirable that seamlessness
among work media is achieved. Users must be able to move smoothly between new multimedia groupware technology and existing single-user single-
medium software. At least there must be a way to exchange documents
with single-user single-medium applications such as Microsoft Word, xfig,
vi, emacs, CorelDraw, FrameMaker, etc.. On the other hand, transitions
between activities, such as brainstorming, outlining, editing, reviewing, storing, communicating, etc. should be transparent and easy, since they do not
always occur in a sequential manner.

The ability to work simultaneously on a shared surface helps people to
communicate, since more work can be done in parallel. Bly (see [Bly et al. 90])
observed people interacting in design sessions and indicated that most drawing events occurred on regions of the drawing that were shared. To support
this, the users should be allowed to work simultaneously over shared objects
of each medium (text characters, pixels, graphical primitives, video frames,
etc.). Different co-authors should be able to select from different tools and
different objects, and perform different commands at the same time. In addition, their views of the information should be the same (as long as they are
"looking" at the same portion of the scrolled windows), i.e. only the editing
space is shared identically between all co-authors.

The tool should provide all co-authors with concurrent access to the editing space. Concurrent access should be allowed to the point of being able
to work on the same drawing at the same time. In the same way, it should
allow them to work on close video frames or to edit the same text sentence.
In Sect. 4.1.3 we refer to some possibilities that can be offered to co-authors.
When there is concurrent access to shared objects, be it 2D-graphics, text,
video frames or other media, parallelism control is needed to mediate access
to the objects. Parallelism can be achieved by implementing strategies of
locking the objects, often dependent of the medium. In Sect. 5.5 we describe
the cooperative algorithm and architecture to enable this.

All interactive systems, such as word processors and drawing tools, must
provide the ability to undo changes by a user. Undoing, however, becomes
difficult when there are interleaved changes originating from different co-
authors. The undo action in CoMEdiA (in the text, raster images and 2D-
object-oriented graphics media) provides for a global undo: the last change
made by anyone to a chapter is undone. Moreover, the undo action is dependent on the chapter in which it is performed, i.e. at each time point as many

different undo actions are possible as there are different chapters. CoMEdiA does not support individual undoing.

Viewing, gesturing, editing, etc. should be independent of each other in the sense that they should be possible at any time and in any temporal sequence. Each co-author should be able to perform any action independently of the existence of other co-authors and of what they are doing (exception made for access conflicts). In order to minimise overhead encountered when storing information (which is a rather time-intensive and not an interactive operation), the co-authors should not be blocked when one of them saves a chapter. They should be able to continue private, as well as cooperative, work while the information is being saved.

Our experience shows that typical editing sessions involve two to three participants. It is still unclear for us whether this will remain so for computer-supported editing sessions (because people will no longer have the problem of physically accessing the editing surface - board, paper). Because of this, it is a goal of CoMEdiA not to support any number of simultaneous co-authors but rather small groups (1 to 6 participants). This limitation is also due to limited computational power, limited code optimisation time and the need for good response times.

4.4 Multimedia Communication

The purpose of this Sect. is to examine the ideas behind the use of multi-media communication within a work group. Recent research has been concerned with the efficiency and effectiveness of information exchange in work groups that use computer technology to meet supported by non-multimedia and multimedia communication channels. Computer-supported multimedia communication has been portrayed in vendor and popular publications as a technological marvel for increasing group information and productivity. We would like to investigate whether this idea is correct and also examine the premise that computer-supported multimedia communication is a complex but fundamentally understandable intervention in interpersonal interaction which systematically alters group processes and behaviour.

It is also important to investigate whether a potential increase in media, media combination or bandwidth does result in an overall increase in communication (implying information overflow). It may be important because of the different functionalities (e.g. ephemeral vs. non-ephemeral), to have different communication channels and media.

4.4.1 Face-to-face Meetings: Advantages and Disadvantages

As one of the purposes of this work is to show how face-to-face meetings can be supported by using multimedia communication and to prove the necessity of the type of communication that occurs in face-to-face meetings we will characterise them with some observations.

The following observations explain the persistent desirability of face-to-face meetings. If these characteristics are so desirable and commonly accepted, then they should be embodied in other media for communication. Face-to-face meetings provide:

- Optimal response time, where there are no delays due to the media, permitting a synchronisation of utterances and turn-taking;

- Non-verbal responses which indicate a range of reactions such as understanding, disbelief, irritation and so on. The opportunity for immediate feedback to an utterance is extremely important, and it is part of the reason why meetings are the medium for selling, persuading, negotiating and so on;

- Social context which provides a vehicle for peer pressure (conformity), risk-taking behaviour, domination (e.g. talking more loudly than someone else, or sitting in the "proper seat"), collective identity (team spirit), rituals (e.g. recognition and awards by a group) and so on;

- Spontaneity of contribution where an attendee signals and then presents a reaction to the latest contribution to the conversation. In work settings, spontaneous interactions via hallway encounters and so on serve a similar purpose, providing peaceful exchange;

- The opportunity for socialisation, which is important even in the most task-oriented meetings through joking, comradeship and so on. In some cases, a user need is satisfied by a glance of acknowledgement or recognition;

- A shared physical setting, including the visual surfaces (white boards, etc.) room arrangement, furniture and so on;

- Remote meetings make group focus more difficult, requiring more concentration. Users usually comment that face-to-face meetings feel shorter, seem to accomplish more in less time and are frequently more exhilarating. In contrast, remote sessions tend to require more concentration and are more tiring. Since discussion is more difficult when some of the group members are distant, people appear to work harder (i.e. they make a conscious effort) to get and give feedback.

Even though the importance of socialisation cannot be underestimated, face-to-face meetings also have serious disadvantages, i.e. geographically dispersed groups also offer benefits. They include:

- Face-to-face meetings have the inconvenience of having to be in the same place and time, which requires inordinate scheduling effort, to say nothing of travel;

- When face-to-face meetings are not scheduled (e.g. spontaneous) they become a major source of lost productivity due to interruptions;

- In face-to-face meetings each person waits for a chance to speak, and contributions are often lost because the appropriate moment has passed. Turn-taking is subject to variables, many of which result from political and social factors rather than task content ([Kerr et al. 92]).

- Dispersed groups have access to the best available expertise, where it may otherwise be logistically impractical or expensive;

- Dispersed groups have access to a specific technological environment (e.g. the technical team of a specialist supplier) where local knowledge of availability and practicality is of key importance;

- Dispersed groups have access to a rich information environment, where additional specialist information may be obtained as the need arises during the meeting (cf. the requirement that we take with us what we think we will need to a face-to-face meeting so as not to constrain its progression; participants who stay in their offices during the non-face-to-face meetings have access to their local books and files). This sometimes allows easy access to important information that would otherwise not be available. Convenience, comfort and familiarity associated with remaining in one's own office is therefore an advantage of remote meetings;

- Remote meetings encourage parallel work within the group. People often divide into subgroups to work on different parts of a document during an editing session. This is also done in face-to-face sessions, but not as frequently as in distributed sessions. Also, it is easy for participants in a remote meeting to drop out for a while, do something else (have a coffee), then return. This is not socially acceptable in most face-to-face situations;

- Remote meetings cut down on social interaction. They tend to be more serious. Since there is less interchange about non-task-related topics, people tend to focus on the task immediately. The effect is a possible efficiency gain in terms of time saved and a possible loss from the aspect of social needs.

Face-to-face meetings are all too often the medium of choice because people are experienced with that medium and feel comfortable with it. Applications to support CSCW should try to use multimedia techniques - insofar as user-communication and information expressiveness are required - to meet user needs currently served by face-to-face meetings while avoiding the disadvantages.

Furthermore, we can itemize the following evidence:

- Face-to-face meetings are still the dominant "medium" of communication as well as the largest single activity for office workers. They consume 25% to 35 % the average office worker's time and up to 70% of an executive's time;

- Face-to-face meetings are the most desirable medium of communication despite of the enormous difficulties of scheduling and efficiency;

- Proximity is the major determinant of working relationships. For example, Kraut (see [Kraut et al. 88]) found that the percentage of people collaborating drops from 10.3% on the same office corridor to 1.9% on the same floor. Essentially, proximity makes meetings, especially informal encounters, easier;

- Tele-conferencing, which most closely approximates meetings, has not penetrated much into the market over the 20 years since its inception (see [Egido 89]). Video-conferencing has become a synonym for marketing disaster. In fact, video does not add much to communication, as concluded by several studies. Vendors are still pushing tele-conferencing despite its low use, arguing that lower costs will make it attractive;

- Despite the telephone's world-wide ubiquity, average usage is about 15% of an office worker's time. Users have adapted well to the limits of telephone communication.

4.4.2   The Necessity of Having Multimedia Communication Channels

Here we will not only look at the necessity of communication channels, but also at the necessity for these channels to convey multimedia information. When people are physically close to each other, communication typically occurs through face-to-face meetings. Compared with other communication channels, face-to-face communication is socially oriented and rich. From a media richness perspective, visually-oriented face-to-face communication is a rich medium that is interactive (providing opportunity for timely feedback and for tailoring of messages to personal circumstances) and expressive (having the ability to convey multiple cues and to use language variety). Hence, it should be useful to increase understanding and reduce the amount of uncertainty in a given communication situation by simulating the face-to-face channel.

These properties and the analyses of early experiments (see [Fish et al. 92]) using video to support distributed work suggest that audio and video channels might provide the basis for the informal communication present in face-to-face meetings when supporting remote meetings. Below we review the reasoning based on the literature, suggesting that a visual channel with audio is helpful in:

- Increasing the spontaneity and frequency of communication;

- Supporting social relationships;

- Coping with the most complex and equivocal communication problems encountered in work groups;

- Integrating members into and supporting the work in work groups.

In situations where groups meet to edit information, different aspects of communication behaviour are of interest for discussion. The following examines the reasons for using a certain type of channel, a certain media combination, the effects of the channels and so on.

Participation of group members: refers to the distribution of communication in the group. In many groups, participation is unequal, and the proportion of participation is predicted by group members' social position and personal competencies. For example, signs of people's external status elicit status generalisation, the tendency for group members to respond to the external status of a group member. Non-multimedia communication lacks mechanisms for displaying or enforcing social differentiation among people. The loss of this differentiating social information might reduce the social influence function of communication (compared with face-to-face communication). Our reasoning is that if the communication focuses attention on non-multimedia media, and if it fails to communicate differentiating social cues such as high external status, then participation and satisfaction during the editing sessions will diminish.

Interpersonal behaviour: refers to the expressive behaviour which is, or seems to be, affective in tone (such as insulting, laughing, shouting) and is relevant to such issues as how a group deals with conflict and whether it promotes uninhibited or antisocial group behaviour. The relative absence of social context information and social feedback in computer-mediated communication (especially non-multimedia) might lead to uninhibited behaviour because these gaps are not replaced by shared norms for conveying or interpreting the social meaning of what is communicated. The more communication depends on text (or other "poorly communicative" media), and the less multimedia channels are used, the more depersonalisation results. We believe that computer-mediated multimedia communication, as opposed to face-to-face communication, will reduce feelings of embarrassment, guilt and empathy for the others; produce less social comparison with others; and reduce fears of retribution or rejection. This technologically induced *de-individuation* should lead to more uninhibited behaviour in cooperative editing systems or, in general, computer-supported cooperative systems.

Consensus development: is the process of resolving conflicts so as to permit a group decision. Decisions in computer-mediated groups are more volatile than decisions in face-to-face ones.

Turn frequency and duration: As shown by several previous studies mediating conversations with multimedia technology appeared to have no discernible effects on the number of turns taken per session, the average length of those turns, or on the distribution of the turns among speakers. These results contrast with other findings considering audio channels only. When just audio channels are available turn length tends to increase relative to face-to-face meetings.

Simultaneous speech and floor control: People reported more difficulty in taking control of a meeting when they used a video channel than when they met face-to-face. Also, differences emerge in the amount of simultaneous speech that occurs and the time between switching speakers. Higher percentages of the time are occupied by only one participant. In asking what may be inferred from this drop in simultaneous speech, we have to explain what function simultaneous speech can serve. It may indicate problems with the floor control mechanism (it is not completely clear to the participants when they can/should speak). It can also mean that the degree of interaction and spontaneity in the meeting is high.

The possibility of simultaneous communication relaxes many constraints during the editing process, and increases the possible bandwidth of communication in editing meetings. In ordinary meetings, the meaning of what is said often depends on the context of what was said just before. If multiple things can be "said" (said, seen written, and so on) at once in the prototype system, it can be argued that such capacities introduce confusion in the meeting process. On the other hand, this capability can be enormously liberating in the context of a fast-moving brainstorming session. Reading is faster than listening, so it is possible to scan the items being created by several others and occasionally respond to them. When something puzzling comes along on the screen, however, it is not necessary to attend to it at once. Unlike oral communication, there is no need to remember a confusing item, because it remains on the screen for later processing. A written communication channel or a written common workspace is thus useful because it is non-ephemeral and allows the possibility of later systematic processing. Thus, a potential increase in bandwidth (and media) does not result in an overall increase in communication (implying information overflow); it may be important for the reason of their different functionality.

Frequency and spontaneity of interaction: The presence of a visual and audio channel is important in initiating communication in a remote meeting (especially informal communication), as well as increasing the probability of interaction. They help in the identification of participants, topics, moments of interaction, engagement and so on (see [Fish et al. 92]).

4.4.3   Desirable Goals and Objectives of Multimedia Communication

To the extent that audio and video communication simulates the features of face-to-face communication in being expressive and interactive and focusing attention on personal attributes, it should function as face-to-face communication. Thus, the media richness and tele-presence perspective suggest that audio and video channels should be well suited for informal communication, and especially good for aiding the more social, the more uncertain, and the more equivocal aspects of communication. For example, the evidence from early studies suggests that audio and video channels, face-to-face meetings or written exchanges are of roughly equivalent value for information transfer tasks, but are differentiated when consensus formation and conflict are at issue (see [Fish et al. 92]).

From previous research we can infer that non-multimedia communication might reduce communication efficiency. In the first place, typing and reading is more difficult than speaking and listening. Second, inhibiting the flow of social feedback, feelings, and social meanings decreases the efficiency of interpersonal communication. For example, not being able to nod one's head to indicate understanding or to murmur 'humm' impedes one's ability to communicate comprehension of the other person's message efficiently.

Based on our experience with supporting multimedia communication channels, and on the previous Sect., we propose the following as desirable goals for our cooperative multimedia editing prototype tool (which are general enough to be also considered for group decision support systems, computer-mediated communication systems, electronic meeting systems, coordination systems and so on):

- Individuals do not deal with problems only when they meet together as a group. Nor do they operate as only one group. Groups are very fluid, overlapping and intersecting. Any tool needs to offer the flexibility to be used synchronously and asynchronously;

- Individual and group editing requirements imply that the tool must integrate computer resources of several media with the communication channels as part of the work process;

- Privacy, security and reliability of human communication are essential for system acceptance;

- It should be clear how easy it can be to reach others using the communication channels;

- Individuals have a great deal of freedom in their work as to what mode of communication they will use for what purpose. A determined communication technology cannot be imposed on them;

- The members must have sufficient cues to be confident to groups; of the interpretations the other are giving to their actions;

- The members must have means available to clarify and enforce commitments and expectations;

Other aspects that must be considered and included in the tool are:

- Groups using multimedia communication channels will exchange fewer remarks, and will take longer to reach consensus, than they will using face-to-face communication. However, a higher proportion of the discussion remarks are task-oriented and explicit decision proposals;

- Group members will participate more equally in group discussions than will group members engaged in face-to-face information processing;

- Uninhibited behaviour will occur more frequently using multimedia communication;

- Group choices different from initial individual choices will be more frequent with multimedia channels than in face-to-face situations;

- Multimedia channels diminish simultaneous speech and the time between switching speakers;

- Multimedia channels increase the probability of initiating communication in a remote meeting;

- Multimedia channels are the most suited for informal communication, especially for aiding the social, uncertain and equivocal aspects of communication.

4.4.4   Video Communication

There are important differences between video and face-to-face meetings, some of which are rather obvious. Unlike eyes, cameras have a fixed field of view and usually cannot be controlled by the viewer. Failure to make eye contact also tends to be a problem because of the separation of camera and monitor. In video-mediated meetings, the principle of reciprocity does not always hold (i.e. if I can see you, you can see me). There is no concept of a negotiated mutual distance between speakers, and they have no sense of how their voices are perceived by listeners. Other differences are more subtle and hard to define, such as relative impotence of gestures and gaze in securing others' attention through video, and the feeling of being "distant" from others.

Many of these problems are compounded when one is restricted to a single camera and monitor in order to converse with multiple parties. One way of supporting multiparty conversations is to use different windows for different participants. However, when multiple participants occupy a single screen, participants are limited in their ability to: direct their gaze to various participants; be aware of who, if anyone, is visually attending to them; selectively listen to different, parallel conversations; make asides to other participants. The value of video is three-fold. supports non-verbal signals; transmits object information; this may, however, imply high resolution of the images; conveys non-verbal information and situational awareness necessary for critical group processes, such as getting to know each other or conflict resolution. This seems to make a very strong case for developing (bilateral) video-phones, multi-point video networks or video-conferencing systems.

However, for many cases none of the three classes of information referred to above is necessary; they might even be harmful. It has been shown that simple brainstorming is better done when the group members or participants do not see each other than in face-to-face meetings (see [McGrath 84]). This conclusion agrees with the finding that asynchronous interaction through e-mail is well suited for idea generation because this induces more equal participation. In many cases adding a video channel to an audio channel will not therefore add much "functionality" to the interaction. This explains the reported result that users prefer improving the audio channel (e.g. larger bandwidth) over adding a video channel or improving it. On the other hand, in a multi-point conferencing setting Galegher (see [Galegher et at. 90a]) found that a video channel was seen as particularly effective when the attention of the group was assesed. Typically, this involved seeing what conditions the others were in, (e.g. in the room, in front of the camera). In this case a video channel supported situational awareness information exchange.

Although gestures and motions transmitted over a video channel do not leave behind any persistent record in the drawing space, we suggest that they can be used to store information. Our experience during this work revealed that co-authors did not experience any problems in remembering gestures later in the editing session or even in later sessions. One aid to remembering is for other co-authors to imitate a gesture. Gestures and movements transmitted via a video channel are particularly well-suited to demonstrate a sequence of actions, such as how a person would interact with a proposed machine or piece of software. Movements are also used to mediate the group's interaction. Pointing to locations often directs the group's attention to a common location, and subtle cues from gestures (e.g. waving a hand to take the turn to talk) can help the group negotiate the use of a shared drawing space. These mediating gestures are usually unremarkable and typically do not add new information by themselves.

4.4.5   Audio Communication

As exposed above (over most of the Sect. 4.4) voice communication is mostly
important for the communication during an editing session. Moreover, it is
known that telephone calls comprise about 20% of the workday interactions,
and that face-to-face meetings account for an additional 25-50%. The hypo-
thetical loss (from face-to-face meetings to remote computer-supported ones)
of speech information is most striking, given this dominance of the audio
medium in influencing communication outcomes regardless of the presence
of visual media. Furthermore, as stated above, speech communication fulfils
different communicative purposes than text and video communication and is
especially valuable for the more complex and controversial aspects of a collaborative task. On one hand, given the ubiquity of telephones we could assume
that a voice channel is always available. Nevertheless, telephone costs are
extra to the network use and can be high (in case of geographically distant
sessions). Also, in a co-author's room there is commonly just one telephone
(also in a terminal room), and it is uncomfortable to have it busy during the
whole duration of the session (which can last for hours). Because of this, extra audio channels, embedded in the tool itself, should be provided. This way
the dynamic creation and destruction of voice channels should be supported.

The value of audio channels appears to be in the transmission of two forms
of interpersonal information: linguistic and para-linguistic. Both content
and relational meaning can therefore be transmitted (as any intensive telephone user knows). Because of the many types and meanings of information
transmitted, audio channels can support both task and group maintenance
contents. However, the transfer of non-verbal signals and visual object information is not possible, and situational awareness information is conveyed
only to a limited extent. This implies that tasks involving object-related
discussions can hardly be done with audio channels alone.

4.4.6   Text Communication

Text is the communication medium that seems less expressive and interesting. One of the questions that is frequently posed is whether communication
through a text channel alone reduces coordination of communication. In
traditional forms of communication, head nods, smiles, eye contact, distance,
tone of voice and other non-verbal behaviour give speakers and listeners information they can use to regulate, modify and control information exchanges.
Electronic communication, in general, may be inefficient for resolving such
coordination problems as telling another person one already knows what he
wants to explain. Also, text communication is very depersonalising. Because
without even the texture of paper to lend printed text individuality, electronic communication tends to seem impersonal. It might be especially hard
to communicate liking or intimacy, without writing unusually positive text.

Text channels also have positive aspects. The communication is non-ephemeral, i.e. the information transmitted is not lost as it is output. For example, with an audio channel, if a co-author listens to something he wants to remember later it has to be converted to an other medium in order to be used later (e.g. written in an annotation, drawn). Very often a co-author notices that what another co-author said minutes before would be useful at that moment. Nevertheless, it is impossible to retrieve it. The same happens with video communication. A way to overcome this problem would be to record the contents of the audio and of the video channel. Unfortunately, this is impossible in practice because of the size of the recordings. As an example, 10 minutes of audio and video communication can amount to 80 Mbyte. Another advantage is that a text channel does not need a high bandwidth from the network (because it is interactive) nor does it require high software complexity or software development time (such as an audio or a video channel). Also, the social effects of text communication have been well studied and documented and produce less co-author inhibition.

4.4.7   Implicit Communication

A key advantage in the process of creating and using drawings, text and any other medium is the timing of activities among co-authors. Expressing ideas or mediating interaction sometimes involves several people working together synchronously in the drawing space. This cooperative editing process of building on and interactively developing representations for ideas and concepts in the editing space often involves fine-grained interactions in time among the co-authors. Timing a gesture or drawing with a verbal explanation of it, or timing an activity to coordinate with the activity of other co-authors are important uses of implicit ways of communication not included in any communication mechanism on its own. It is in part this familiar sense of implicit communication that enables the group to coordinate the highly engaged, cooperative activities. Drawbacks to timing are the possible processing and transmission delays that cause the objects being edited in the common edit spaces to fall out of synchrony from the accompanying verbal explanation and video gestures.

In face-to-face meetings, one key advantage that a group uses to help mediate interaction is a close physical proximity among the members. This proximity allows a peripheral awareness of the other participants and their actions. Many intricate and coordinated actions can be observed in this kind of meeting (such as avoiding collisions with other hands) that demonstrate an awareness of the other participants, enabled by being in close proximity with them. By having concurrent access to the editing space, the co-authors can work in parallel, easing bottlenecks (such as the time it takes to store information) or reducing the competition for conventional turn-taking, since other people can work in the shared drawing space while one person is talking or using other media. However, this increased parallelism can be a problem because it makes it harder to keep a shared focus as a group. Thus, concurrent

access in the context of implicit communication can be a problem at times
as well as an advantage.

4.5   Evaluation of the Technology-level Factors

Following what was explained in Sect. 3.2, we give here the advantages
and disadvantages of each of the technology-level factors (TF), and propose
an evaluation schedule attributing value to the several effects and benefits.
Based on these we then evaluate the value of the input factors.

Mapping the referred group coordination effects (CE) to the tangible
group benefits we obtain the table below. This table shows that the group coordination effects that could lead to the most group benefits (assuming equal
weights[2]) are: greater participation by co-authors (CE.2:4), increased access
to information (CE.8:4), increase in the level of parallel activity (CE.1:3),
synergy among workers (CE.5:3) and greater coordination of group work
(CE.9:3). By concentrating on the group coordination effects that produce
greatest benefits, we will increase the likelihood that their innovations will
be accepted by industry.

	Time	Output	Satisfaction/efficiency	Other	Total
CE.1	•		•	•	3
CE.2	•	•	•	•	4
CE.3	•				1
CE.4	•				1
CE.5	•	•		•	3
CE.6		•			1
CE.7		•			1
CE.8	•	•	•	•	4
CE.9	•		•	•	3

The next table relates technology-level factors to total group benefits,
and each dot denotes a value equal to its benefit expressed in the previous table. The value 186 is the maximum of group benefits an application
can have following the evaluation strategy. From here we conclude that the
technology-level factors that induce most benefits are WYSIWIS and synchronous updates (TF.5:21), concurrent data access (TF.6:18), multimedia
editing (TF.13:14), private annotations and public comments (TF.8:14), multimedia communication (TF.14:13), multiple-cursors, tele-pointing and gesturing (TF.4:13) and brainstorming (TF.1:13).

The column on the far right represents numerically the total group benefits that each technology-level factor brings. The total group benefits of each
mechanism is expressed below left. The bottom line represents numerically

---

[2]This is assumed for simplification as different weights for each of the group coordination
effects would be very difficult to assume correctly given the diversity of possible uses and
users.

the total group benefits that all technology-level factors bring. The total group benefits of all technology-level factors is is expressed below right.

$$\sum_{j=1}^{9} CE.j \qquad\qquad \sum_{i=1}^{17}\sum_{j=1}^{9} TF.i \times CE.j$$

From this table it is possible to rank these features (technology-level factors), making it clear which must be implemented first and in the highest degree (the 9 CEs in the columns and the 17 TFs in the rows):

	1 (3)	2 (4)	3 (1)	4 (1)	5 (3)	6 (1)	7 (1)	8 (4)	9 (3)	
1	•	•			•				•	13
2	•			•						4
3		•			•				•	10
4		•		•	•	•	•		•	13
5	•	•	•	•	•	•	•	•	•	21
6	•	•	•	•	•	•	•	•		18
7			•	•		•			•	6
8	•	•			•			•		14
9		•			•					7
10	•			•				•		8
11			•			•			•	5
12				•		•			•	7
13	•	•	•			•	•	•		14
14		•		•	•	•	•		•	13
15	•	•		•	•					11
16			•			•	•	•	•	10
17	•	•		•				•		12
Maximal group benefits of all technology-level factors										186

Chapter 5

The Prototype Tool - CoMEdiA

> *"Any tool that is built to be sold in some way is a result of compromise."*

One of the difficulties of implementing a cooperative multimedia editing tool is that it implies solving problems on diverse fields, namely distributed systems, multi-user interfaces, media integration, communication and human factors.

CoMEdiA - Cooperative hyperMedia Editing Architecture is an architecture intended to support and encourage cooperation among several authors, multimedia communication and multimedia editing (see [Hornung et al. 91a, Santos 92a, Santos 93d, Santos 93b]). CoMEdiA is designed to support small groups of up to 6 co-authors working in possibly different locations (connected over a LAN or WAN) who wish to collaborate (but not compete) in order to produce a final document. We assume that each co-author works towards a goal of common interest, supports the other co-authors and promotes the progress of the group. Examples of documents to be produced this way are multimedia documents, which involve people with different backgrounds: scientific reports, newspaper articles, project proposals, source code production, design of rendering scenes for publicity, animation scripts or several kinds of object modelling (see [Santos 93a]). The advantages of groups are that individuals with very different expertise, background, problem approaches and geographic separation can contribute to the problem solution. The potential for a cooperative system such as CoMEdiA lies in the ability to allow people to do this and to integrate the results for the group as a whole.

We intended to realise a system to diminish the costs and restrictions associated with face-to-face communication and the demand for synchronous availability. We built a flexible array of features which are "open" and can be used and combined, according to the characteristics of the problem to be solved or the goal to be achieved. Owing to the several communication modalities supported it allows the information exchange capacity that other cooperative editors and computer-mediated communication systems (e-mail or tele-conferencing) lack. The prototype tool is intended to enable co-authors to work in the same room (face-to-face) or at remote sites within a LAN or a WAN. Following the classification of Figs. 2.2 and 2.3 we characterise CoMEdiA in Fig. 5.1.

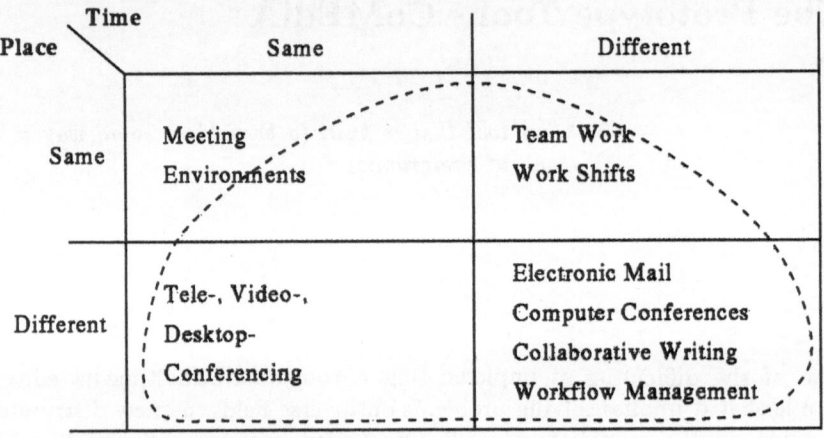

Fig. 5.1: The Johansen Time/Place matrix showing the area for which CoMEdiA has been designed

In Sects. 5.1, 5.2, 5.3 and 5.4 we describe in detail the implementation features of the CoMEdiA prototype tool. CoMEdiA does not impose a barrier between "individual" and "group" ways of working. For example, it provides co-authors with ready access to their individual work and allows them to import it to the cooperative editing session. CoMEdiA supports a balanced set of features for editing of multimedia documents. It has most usual single-user editing functionalities so as not to overload the co-author with features it is not used to use (as for editing purposes). Synchronous communication is supported by means of an audio channel, a video channel, a text channel, the WYSIWIS technique, the public comments, the co-author individual and global information. Asynchronous communication is supported in the sense that co-authors can work independently of each other's presence in the editing session. The CoMEdiA prototype tool provides the communication facilities on which to build the several communication channels. It is easy for the co-authors to establish, use and end a communication channel.

Most groupware, especially for geographically distributed editing sessions, requires an architecture and an algorithm to manage the cooperation where multiple (perhaps distributed) processes can communicate with each other.

In Sect. 5.5 the algorithm and architecture used are explained. These are hybrid approaches of centralised and replicated techniques. The data is replicated over all co-author workstations and there is a central process responsible for the synchronisation and concurrency control. The central process receives user requests for operations and broadcasts them to all users in the editing session. Since the same operations are performed in the same order for all users, all copies of the data remain coherent.

5.1 Multi-user Interface

5.1.1 Multiple-cursors, Tele-pointing and Gesturing

The CoMEdiA prototype system supports multiple-cursors, tele-pointing and gesturing. In the login of a session each co-author chooses a different cursor (Fig. 5.6). Multiple-cursors are, therefore, unique, each identifying the co-author who chosen it. The selected cursor is continuously visible to the other co-authors so that co-authors are aware of what is being done by all the members of the group (only the cursors that fall in the same screen are drawn, i.e. the ones that are visible for that co-author). As we noted that multiple-cursors added to the use of tele-pointers can lead to over-information and over-complexity of the user interface, there is a mechanism to express which co-authors' cursors can be seen (see Fig. 5.2).

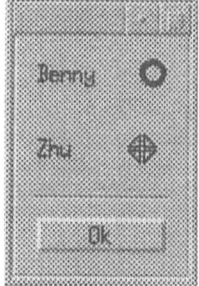 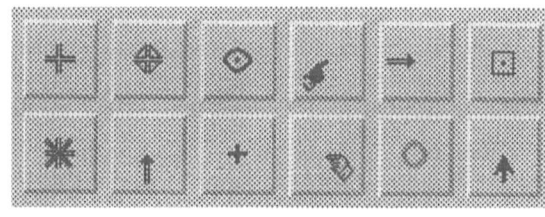

Fig. 5.2: The co-author (left) can see the cursors, in this editing session, of co-authors "Benny" and "Zhu", the cursor of co-author "Adelino" has been disabled. On the right, examples of personalised cursors that can be used by co-authors

For the current window systems only single cursors are supported. As a result, multiple-cursors must be implemented independently of the system supplied cursors. Multiple-cursors are implemented by means of XOR operations on the several cursor bitmaps. Each user process keeps a table of the positions of others' cursors (this for each medium chapter). After a move-

ment of a cursor by a co-author in a certain chapter, the coordinates together
with the user id and the chapter id are sent to the server. The server saves
this information and distributes it to the other users. By receiving this information, each of the other users deletes the personalised cursor corresponding
to the co-author that made the movement from the old position, updates his
or her own table and draws the personalised cursor on the new position. This
happens for cursor and mouse movements, keyboard events, etc.. This same
technique is used for tele-pointers.

The ideal situation would be for synchronous full motion of the cursors
and tele-pointers to be supported. Unfortunately, window systems' imple-
mentations produce such effects as "screen flickering" if this is tried. Also,
the limited network bandwidth is a limiting factor. There are several strategies to avoid these two handicaps:

- Pointing: the above algorithm is executed each time a co-author points
  with the mouse (pressing a button) or hits a key. An advantage is
  that only actions that require a mouse button press or a key hit are
  transmitted, but a disadvantage is that the movements might be so
  sudden that the other co-authors do not notice the gestures (possibly
  losing the action and the new cursor position). This is the technique
  used in the CoMEdiA prototype for the editing actions (mouse drawing,
  text key input, video frame editing and so on);

- Limited motion: the same as above, but after receiving a new position
  the process computes several points in between the old and the new position, and then animates the cursor movement through the computed
  interpolation points. Disadvantages are that it can be an expensive
  process of computation and display, and it still does not guarantee that
  the computed path reflects the actual movement of the sender. This
  technique can be applied to low-end networks, but not to low-end processors;

- Full motion: all the cursor positions are transmitted (whether the co-
  author presses a button or not). If the network is fast enough, every
  co-author will see a cursor movement exactly as the sender. The disadvantage is the network display overloading;

- Modified full motion: as above, but not all the events are sent to the
  server. Just every n^{th} event (second or third) is sent. This because
  the full motion techniques overload the network with "unnecessary"
  events. Our experience shows that if we send every third event the
  other co-authors do not lose expressiveness or gesturing capacity. This
  is the technique used in the CoMEdiA prototype for the tele-pointing
  mechanism.

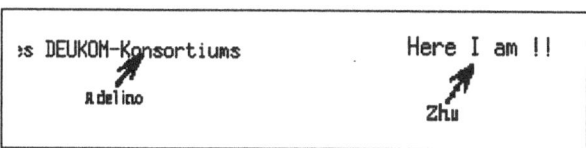

Fig. 5.3: Two examples of tele-pointers of co-authors "Adelino", and "Zhu"

A tele-pointer is a means of directing the attention of the group to a particular document location. It is unique, thus identifying the co-author that manipulates it (by the name it has written). Also, it is prominent because it is bigger than the normal cursors. Both the personalised cursors and the tele-pointers maintain their relative positions on every editing surface so that they retain their meaning and relation to the work objects. The tele-pointer (see Fig. 5.3) must be *picked* and *released*. When a co-author is tele-pointing something, the co-authors that are receiving the tele-pointing are forced to stop what they are doing and passively follow. During the tele-pointing the co-authors that do not tele-point are *frozen* and just watch. As this can be a restrictive tele-pointing mechanism, to improve the functionality there is a selection mechanism (selective tele-pointing) to specify from whom a co-author can receive tele-pointing and to whom a co-author can tele-point. A co-author can choose which co-authors can tele-point to him or her in the "To me" menu, and the co-authors that can be tele-pointed in the "From me" menu. This way, co-author Benny receives tele-pointing from co-author Adelino when Adelino picks the tele-pointer only if Benny is enabled in Adelino's "From me" menu and Adelino is in Benny's "To me".

5.1.2 What You See Is What I See

CoMEdiA offers Relaxed-WYSIWIS from the beginning of an editing session, and the co-authors have the option of toggling to Strict-WYSIWIS. The "Follow (synchronise with) Co-author" feature enforces a situation where two authors are in Strict-WYSIWIS. Co-authors can interchange back and forth between Strict-WYSIWIS and Relaxed-WYSIWIS as they find it advantageous to synchronise their views or have independent perspectives of the document. According to the Relaxed-WYSIWIS concept, a co-author does not have to be watching the same working area as any other in the session. When, because of their own editing necessities, co-authors overlap their its views with each other's, then they can see each other's personalised cursors and editing changes.

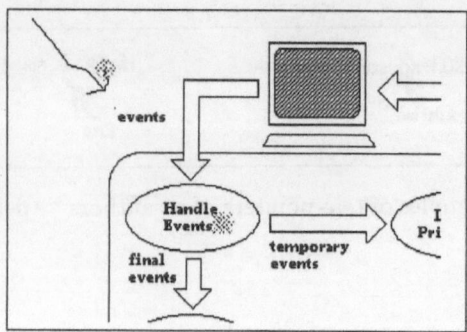

Fig. 5.4: A raster image being edited by three co-authors. The cursors of two of them can be seen: drawing a pointer to the word *events* ("Diamond" form) and writing the word *Handle* ("Star" form)

The social roles of each co-author are used to introduce some control on who can synchronise views with whom. Only a co-author with more rights (higher role) can synchronise with one with fewer. For example, a Reader cannot synchronise with anyone, the Chairperson can synchronise with any co-author and a Commenter cannot synchronise with a Co-author. To control the "Follow (synchronise with) Co-author" feature there are three options: "Begin follow", "End follow" and "Prevent follow".

5.1.3 Access Techniques

There are two different kinds of access techniques (lock mechanisms) generally referred to in the literature (see [Olson et al. 90]): "Chunk Lock" and "Position Lock". In the login window (see Fig. 5.6) the co-author chooses one of them, and if it is not the one being used by the rest of the group then unanimity must be reached. When the Chunk Lock is used, the co-author requests chunks of the document for their own use. This way, there are operation cycles over chunks - Select-Ask-Edit-Free, which can be cumbersome because they require extra actions from the user. With the Position Lock, the co-author locks only the text insertion position, pixel or 2D-graphic primitive to be edited, which is done automatically by the system.

A mechanism for locking objects - characters, character sequences, 2D-primitives, video frames, etc. - is necessary to realise either of these two techniques. In fact, one solution is simply to lock data before it is written. Deadlock or other conflict situations can be prevented by the usual techniques, such as two-phase locking, or by methods more suited to interactive environments. For example, the system might visually indicate locked resources, decreasing the likelihood of requests for these resources (this is what happens in 2D-graphics and video media). Locking presents three problems.

First, the overhead for requesting and obtaining the lock, including wait time if the data is already locked, causes a degradation in response time. Second, there is the question of granularity (for example, Position vs. Chunk). Participants are less constrained as the locking granularity increases, but fine-grained locking adds system overhead. The third problem involves the timing of lock requests or releases. In a text editor the lock can be requested when the cursor is moved or when the key is struck. A system should not burden the user with these decisions, and therefore the locking must be done automatically, if it is possible (e.g. for the Position lock).

More flexible lock mechanisms have been investigated and reported. Tickle locks allow the lock to be released to another requester after an idle period. Soft locks can be broken by explicit override commands. Other schemes notify users when locks are obtained or conflicting requests issued. Other mechanisms could have been used such as transaction mechanisms, dependency detection, reversible execution or operation transformations.

Protocols for *turn-taking* or *floor-passing* can also be used to control the access to documents. Instead of allowing free-for-all at-any-time access, the co-authors have to ask for the "floor" in order to perform any action. The main problem with this technique is that it is limited to those situations in which a single active user fits the dynamics of the session. It is particularly ill-suited for sessions with high parallelism, inhibiting the free and natural flow of information. Additionally, leaving floor control to a social protocol can result in conflicting operations: co-authors often make mistakes in following the protocol or they simply refuse to follow it, and consequently several people act as though they have the right to.

We now give two examples of the Position Lock. In a chapter of the text medium the co-authors can edit only in insertion positions more than a certain distance from any other co-author's insertion position. At the beginning of an editing session this distance has the value of 2 characters. In a chapter of 2D-graphics the co-authors cannot select a graphic primitive that has already been selected by any other co-author.

5.2 Support for Cooperation

5.2.1 Brainstorming Support

The sharing of ideas through the process of parallel sampling from each member is a guard against cognitive inertia, allowing several lines of ideas to run in parallel - even the formation of brainstorming subgroups is possible (see Sect. 4.2.1). The fact that everyone can be entering ideas concurrently overcomes air time and production blocking problems (see Sect. 4.2.1). Unfortunately we do not think CoMEdiA's brainstorming tool can solve the free riding and evaluation apprehension problems.

In CoMEdiA there is a brainstorming board that can be used by any subgroup of co-authors in the editing session (see Fig. 5.5). The co-author must select the option to show it and gets a drawing area that is common to all the other co-authors that also have it shown. The brainstorming then takes place in synchrony with the other co-authors. There is no access conflict control, to improve the performance and responsiveness. Therefore, it can happen that the different boards are not completely coherent. Nevertheless, in our experience it is rare for the boards to get incoherent, and when they do the co-authors hardly notice the difference (mostly it is a matter of pixels). The co-author actions are sent to the server, which distributes them without any checks (completely bypassing the cooperative algorithm - see 5.5) to the other users. The board contents are just recorded in each of the co-authors' sites.

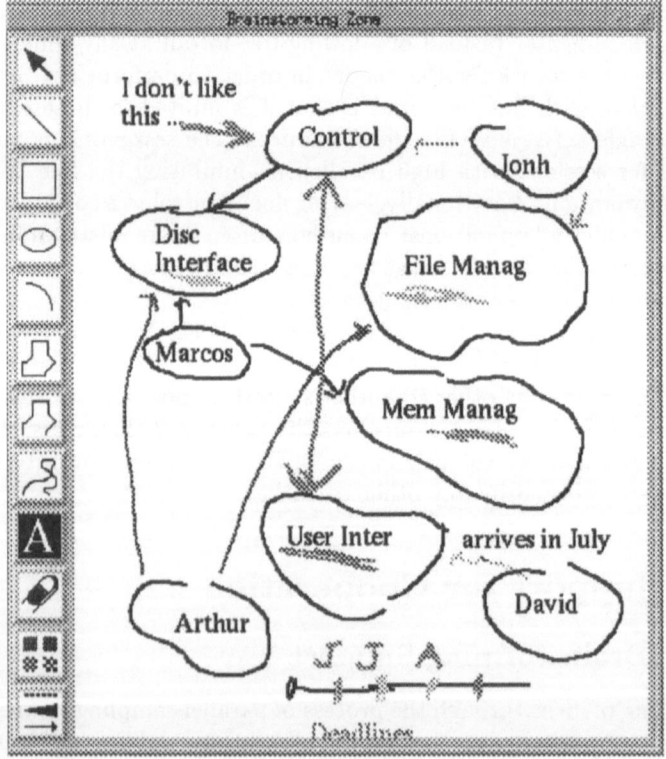

Fig. 5.5: The brainstorming board

The functionalities available are a compromise between expressiveness and ease of use. We think they are enough to express complex concepts. It is possible to express ideas in graphical and textual form, using different primitives, colours and patterns. We have tried to keep it as similar as possible to a single-user tool that would be used by a co-author in private to express the same ideas in a quick, simple and clear form.

5.2.2 Registration Protocol

The registration mechanism (also called "login") allows the user to enter an editing session and to define several parameters that will be used during it. The login window (see Fig. 5.6) enables the user to enter the group name

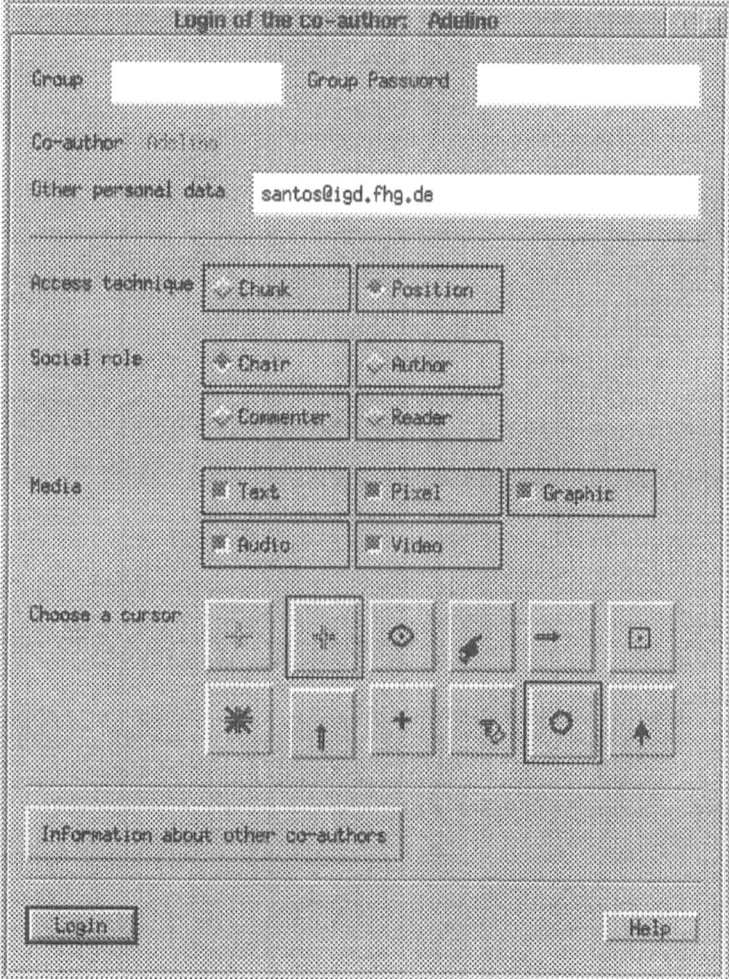

Fig. 5.6: The window to enable the registration process (login window)

and password, diverse information about self, the access technique, the social role, and the personalised cursors and to know which other co-authors are in the editing session.

The personal information, social role and personalised cursor are always recorded so that it can be kept from meeting to meeting. The social role is here checked for coherence (e.g. there cannot be two co-authors with the Chairperson role).

The Chairperson can disable or enable the registration of any of the group members during an editing session. This makes it possible to control the possible access of members, e.g. any whose participation is not desired in a meeting in which a certain matter is being dealt with.

5.2.3   Group Members' Social Roles

Groups are rarely uniform concerning the participants' qualifications, ambitions, expertise, goals, etc.. Several kinds of problems can arise, and one response to these is the definition of social roles. This reduces the coordination problems by specifying *proper behaviours* (responsibilities, permissible actions, restrictions, patterns of interaction) of the group members. Each co-author can choose the social role in the registration process to a session. Any co-author can also have the social role changed during the editing session by the Chairperson. The choice of social role in the registration protocol can depend on several factors, including organisational structure, time constraints, relative social and professional status, skills and expertise of the co-author.

The social roles in CoMEdiA (see Fig. 5.6 and 5.7) are:

- Chairperson: chairs an editing session;

- Author: one of the participants in the meeting who actively contributes to the production of documents;

- Commenter: only empowered to comment on the other co-authors' writings;

- Reader: only empowered to read.

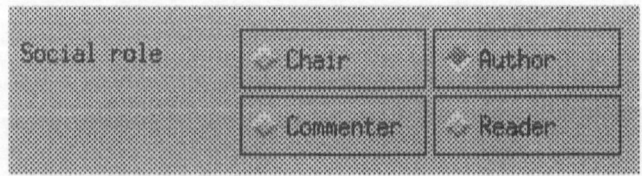

Fig. 5.7: The social roles available to a participant in the registration process

We think these social roles cover most of the situations in cooperative multimedia editing. Nevertheless, other examples can be found, such as:

- Writer: converts ideas into document items, records the document and freely makes changes in the document;

- Consultant: actively participates in different stages of the project but does not really write the information;

- Editor: makes corrections to the information written by someone else, produces the layout and the final document;

- Reviewer: provides comments about the information contained in the document.

The following list shows examples of co-authors' actions within an editing session.

Social role	Co-authors' actions
Chairperson	Manipulate MMDocs
	Enable/disable login of co-authors in an editing session
	Change parameters of editing (e.g. Position Lock size)
	Control the audio capacities (e.g. quality, volume)
	Control the video capacities (e.g. quality, speed)
	Change the Social Role of other co-authors
	Choose a sequential path in the MMDoc (to print or mail)
	Lock a part or a version of a chapter from further editing
Author	Edit inside the several single-medium chapters
	Obtain individual/global information (Session Visualiser)
	Manipulate the hyper-connection in the MMDoc
	Use the Brain-Storming tool
Commenter	Manipulate public comments
	Manipulate private annotations
Reader	Use the communication channels (video, audio, text)
	Modify private parameters (e.g. audio, cursor colours)
	Use "Follow co-author" functionality (strict WYSIWIS)

5.2.4   Private Annotations and Public Comments

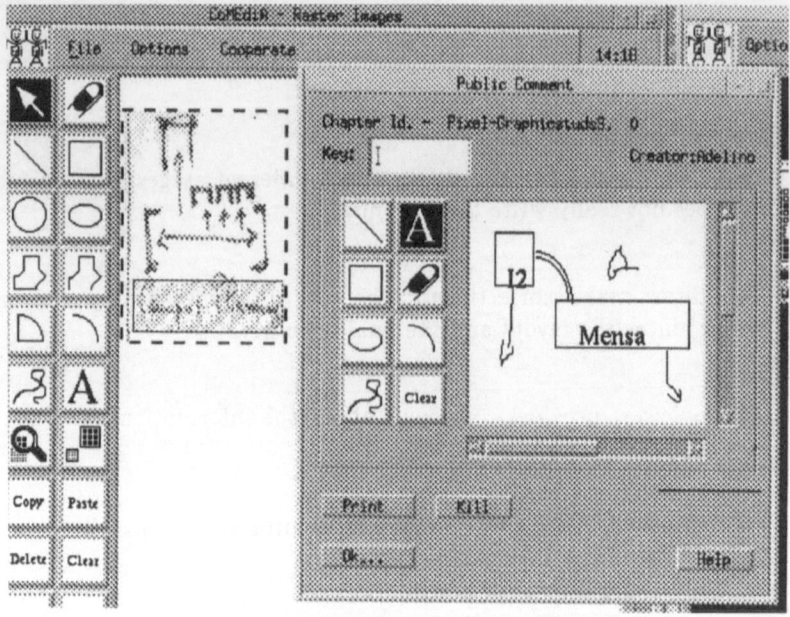

Fig. 5.8: A public comment containing graphical information made on a spot of a raster image. The private annotations have a very similar user interface

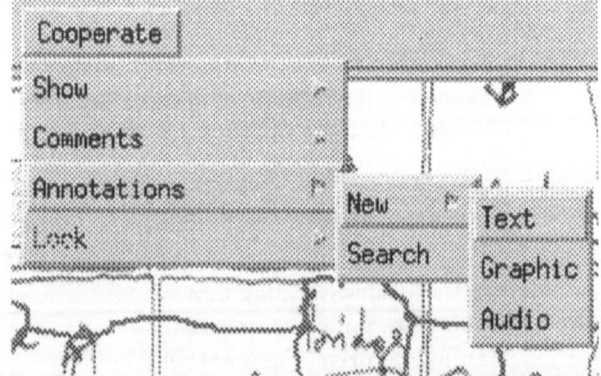

Fig. 5.9: The menu options used to manipulate comments and annotations

A private annotation is an information fragment that refers to a certain spot in the document and expresses an idea about this spot. Its functioning is based on a hypermedia paradigm - it can be accessed following a link and there is a sensitive zone to mark its presence in a spot in the document. It is private in the sense that each co-author maintains his/her own pieces of information that refer to a certain spot in the document. An annotation has a key (given in the creation) that is displayed together with the annotation and can be used for searching. Each annotation can be turned into a public comment. An annotation can contain text, graphic or audio information (see Fig. 5.8 and 5.10). It contains a *mini-editor* with a set of reduced functionalities. In text annotations it is possible to introduce text up to 200 characters long editing it as in a conventional text chapter. In graphic annotations there is the possibility of drawing lines, rectangles, ellipses, free-hands, arcs, text, deleting and clearing areas. The drawing area is small, so that several annotations can be visualised simultaneously (200×300 pixels).

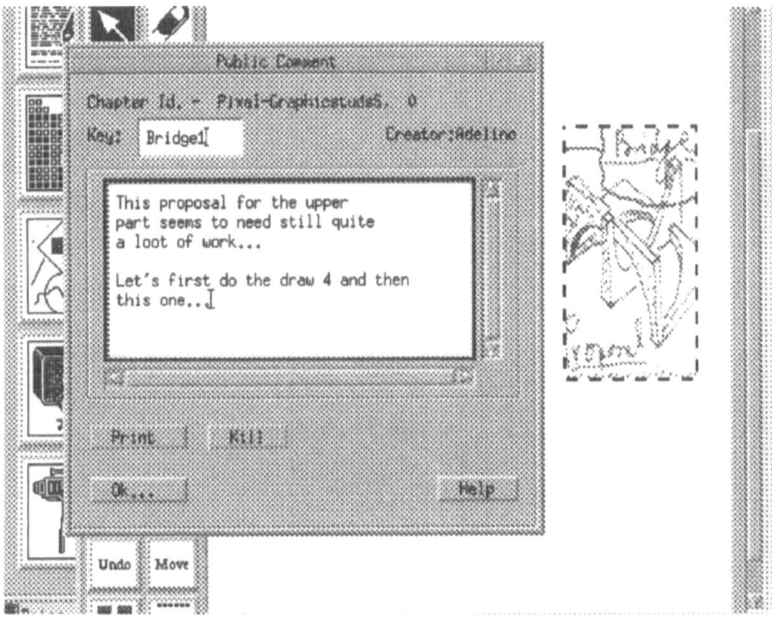

Fig. 5.10: A public comment containing text information made to a spot of a raster image. The private annotations have a very similar user interface

Audio annotations enable the co-author to record, play and cut (pieces of) an audio sequence. For these three functionalities there is the possibility of editing a subsequence that is defined by two mouse clicks or by a textual input time. Annotations are appropriate for private generation of ideas related to those already expressed in a chapter and later communication of these to the group. This *export* action can be realised either by making the annotations public or by means of the intra-group communication mechanisms. The options available are in Fig. 5.9 depict.

Within each annotation, and independently of the annotation medium, there are the options print, kill and make public. Also, diverse information is shown (independently of the annotation medium) together with the annotation window, the identifier, name and medium of the chapter to which the annotation belongs, the annotation key and the creator.

A public comment works in the same way as a private annotation except that the knowledge expressed is common to the whole group. It is public in the sense that it a piece of information common to the group and it is used to explicitly and quickly transmit information to the group (see Fig. 5.8 and 5.10). The options and functionalities available are the same as for private annotations (except the "Make Public") is the information that is displayed within the comment window.

5.2.5   Co-author Information and Awareness

Information and awareness that is passively collected, distributed and presented in the same shared work space as the object is dealt with in Sects.

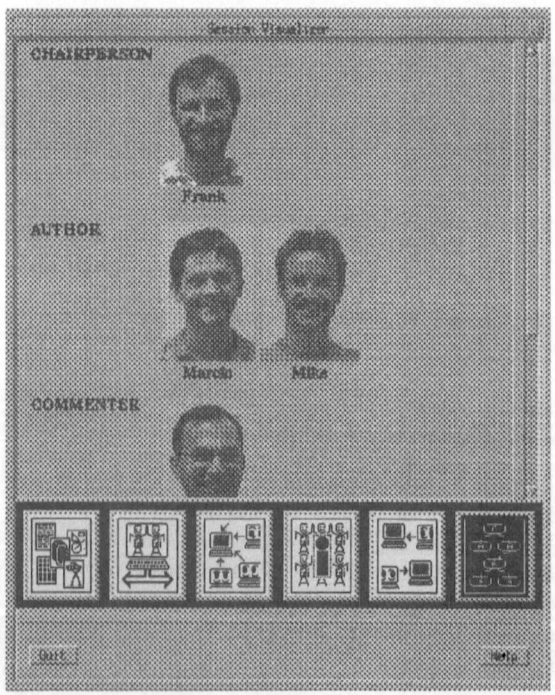

Fig. 5.11: The Session Visualiser window used to display global information about the editing session. The social roles option is shown

5.1.1, 5.1.2, 5.2.3. Information that is explicitly generated, directed and separated from the shared work object can be presented as individual information or as global information.

CoMEdiA can show diverse information about the co-authors, namely name, personal data, cursor used, login time, actual editing position and social role. This information is displayed in a special window whenever the co-author selects the option *Co-authors' information* in the *Cooperate* menu or in the login window (see Fig. 5.12 and 5.6).

To show information about co-authors' interactions and other aspects of the group dynamics there is a window called the "Session Visualiser" (see 5.11). Here is it possible to visualise information about the media used by other co-authors, the communication channels currently in use, the telepointing activities, the individual information, the Strict-WYSIWIS and the social roles of the participants in the editing session.

5.2.6 Support for Latecomers

In CoMEdiA a co-author can start an editing session at any time. Also, other group members can enter the session whenever needed. There are no synchronisation restrictions for the co-authors, i.e. they do not need to alter or stop their work when a new co-author enter the system. The new co-author gets up-dated versions of the documents being edited, as well as information about the co-authors already logged in. Nevertheless, it is not possible to "load" the work of previous editing sessions in order to catch up where they had left off.

5.3 Multimedia Editing

To support seamlessness among the work media an integrated environment is provided. Also, the formats used to store/read/import information are not specific of CoMEdiA. It is possible to exchange data with other single-user editors. The co-authors work in a work space that is common to all participants (for each media chapter) while the tools in use at any moment can vary independently from co-author to co-author.

Viewing, gesturing and editing (writing, drawing, etc.) can be separated from each other in terms of sharing for any of the media considered. It is possible that only one co-author wants to draw at a time, while any other co-author may gesture (move the cursor around the editing windows); similarly, different co-authors may choose to view different parts of the windows in distinct ways (e.g. at different magnifications or at different locations). On the other hand, even if all co-authors are able to edit in different windows simultaneously a co-author may not see the position of every other co-author's cursor.

The input-sharing paradigm for most cooperative editors has usually been *all* or *one*: either any user could edit anywhere on the windows at any time or input was serialised. Unconstrained access is usually limited to pixel-oriented drawing and audio editors, because the editing units (pixel or byte) are too small to be noticed by humans and too many for access to be managed in any efficient way.

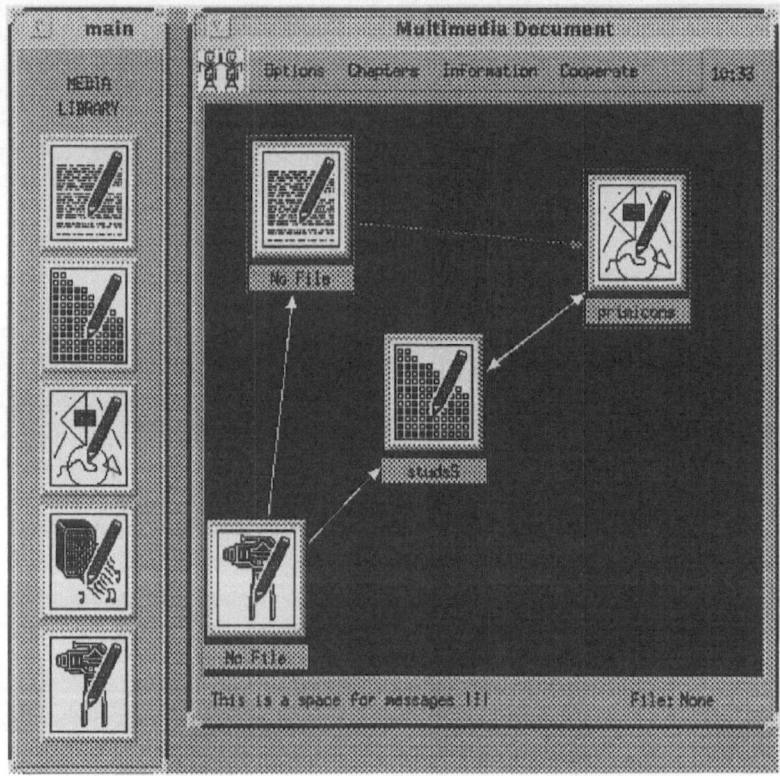

Fig. 5.12: An example of the top-level CoMEdiA user interface

Independently of the media being edited, awareness of others' actions is high and collisions are surprisingly infrequent. Awareness of other co-authors' activities is frequently at a subconscious level. For example, during the brainstorming phase people feel totally occupied with entering their own thoughts as fast as they can. Nevertheless, little duplication of ideas is usually registered (most of the brainstorming items are fresh material when they are presented), so co-authors must have been reading other contributions without being aware of it or investing much time on it. Also, there are usually very few collisions with people working on the same item at the same time. Also, because of the availability of several media and of the cooperation possibilities, editing can become rather confusing, unfocused and chaotic. Many things can be going on at once. Several people may be busy on different chapters of the document, or at different spots of the same chapter.

Fig. 5.12 shows what one co-author working with CoMEdiA sees in the beginning of an editing session. It shows a cooperative editing session in which the multimedia document being processed by the group has 4 chapters (1 with text, 1 with 2D-graphics, and 2 with static images). The organisation of the multimedia document is shown (up left), as are the *Multimedia Library* and the *Multimedia Document* windows. This last is a library of media from where the co-authors can choose the medium (Text, Pixel-images, 2D-Graphics, Audio, and Video are available in the Media Library) for a further chapter of document that they want to create. After choosing the medium they place the new chapter in the multimedia document window and make the connections that relate (connect) this new chapter with the rest of the document. After this step one more chapter of the document exists (although empty), and for editing purposes it must be activated (by clicking in the icon). A Multimedia Document in CoMEdiA is not a sequential bundle of media pieces but rather a hyper organised composite of chapters (each containing one medium). The chapter containing text and one containing 2D-graphics are activated (have a frame around the icon).

For each medium in the Multimedia Library we enable editing by providing an appropriate editor. We have implemented the editors for each

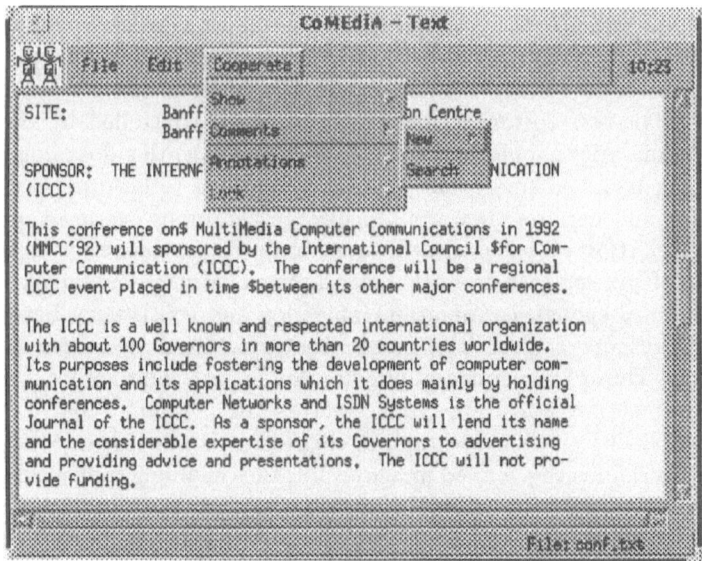

Fig. 5.13: An example of how a text chapter might look

of the media, and not relied upon others already in the market (vi, Mi-croEmacs, FrameMaker, xfig and so on), because of the cross-platform and heterogeneous nature of our work. Another reason is that applications that are written specifically for multiple-users can be multiple-user aware - they can provide customised views and provide information about the conference itself and the roles of the various co-authors. Single-user applications running under "cooperative conditions" (e.g. shared windowing techniques 2.3.1.6) were not written in the anticipation of multiple-users and therefore cannot provide these features. For instance, they could not provide co-authors with a list of the current editing session participants. Typically conference in-formation provided (e.g. tele-pointers) cannot be used by the single-user application made cooperative.

5.3.1   Text Medium

In the text chapters it is possible to edit text files. The editing functionalities available are the customary set common to most single-user editors. The concurrent access is controlled by the server and the granularity is either the text insertion position (when the Position Lock access technique is being used - see 4.1.3) or a chunk. The text is stored in pure ASCCI format in order to be re-usable for single-user editors.

5.3.2   Raster and 2D-Object-oriented-graphics Media

In the raster images chapters it is possible to edit raster images that have previously been acquired by scanning, rendering or any other method, thus enabling continued work on ideas that may have been originated outside Co-MEdiA. The editing functionalities available are the customary set common to most single-user editors. Concurrent access is controlled by the server and the granularity should be the pixel. Nevertheless, this does not happen, because pixels are so small that it is hard for them to be processed by the human eye and because they would cause an enormous overhead in the ac-cesses (a selection of a 10cm×5cm area would cause coherency checking of hundreds of pixels). On the other hand, the algorithm explained in Sect. 5.5 is powerful enough to maintain coherency and consistency between the several co-authors' copies. The images that are edited are stored in "xwd" (X Window Dump) which is a public domain format commonly used. It can be transformed into and from "tiff", "gif", "ppm", "pnm", "eps", etc..

In the 2D-object-oriented-graphics chapters it is possible to edit oriented graphics overlaid with a loaded image or not, thus enabling continued work on ideas that may have been originated outside CoMEdiA. The editing function-alities available are the customary set common to most single-user editors.

Concurrent access is controlled by the server and the granularity is the graphic primitive. To use the Manipulate primitives, the co-author first has to select the object. If this object is already being manipulated by another co-author (and this is stored in the server) then no access is given until the current co-author frees it. The objects are stored in CSS (Central Structure Storage from PHIGS). It is possibile to adjust locations and sizes of objects precisely by means of the ObjectInfo functionality.

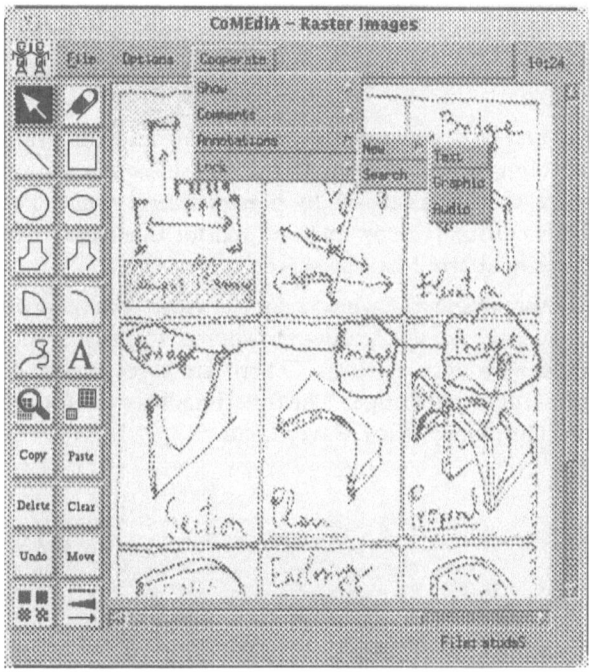

Fig. 5.14: An example of how a raster images chapter might look

5.3.3   Audio Medium

The editing functionalities available are a subset of the customary set common to most single-user editors. We decided to implement audio only as human voice initially; later we will extend the implementation to include music, noises, and so on. We aimed at implementing a tool that would enable co-authors to express ideas as quickly as possible - simplicity of use was preferred to completeness of features.

The functionalities supported are to Record, Play and Cut an arbitrary audio sequence. Any of these three functionalities is activated during a certain amount of time, which can be expressed numerically or by button press. It is possible to add, delete and cut audio from any arbitrary point of the sequence. The audio sequences are stored in a subset of the WAVE format.

5.3.4   Video Medium

In the video chapters it is possible to edit video sequences. The editing functionalities available are a subset of the customary set common to most single-user editors. The video chapters include functionalities to record, edit and play video sequences. We use the IFAV format (Intermidiate Format for Audio and Video, see [Santos 93e, Tritsch et al. 92]) for storing and, as for audio medium, we aimed at implementing a simple and quick-to-use editor to compose video sequences, which would enable co-authors to express ideas as fast as possible.

Concurrent access is controlled by the server and the granularity is one frame. By selecting a sequence of frames (at least one) a co-author locks them. They are then surrounded by a wire frame, which is white for the co-author who is editing (the owner) and red for the others. Any attempt to select red frames is aborted by the server.

In Fig. 5.15 we present the window for the video chapters, which is used to edit a video sequence. All the frames are shown, together with the recording times associated with each of them. There are three modes of marking for editing: Single, Multi and Range. The functionalities to edit are very simple, namely Delete, Cut, Copy, Play, Save, Load.

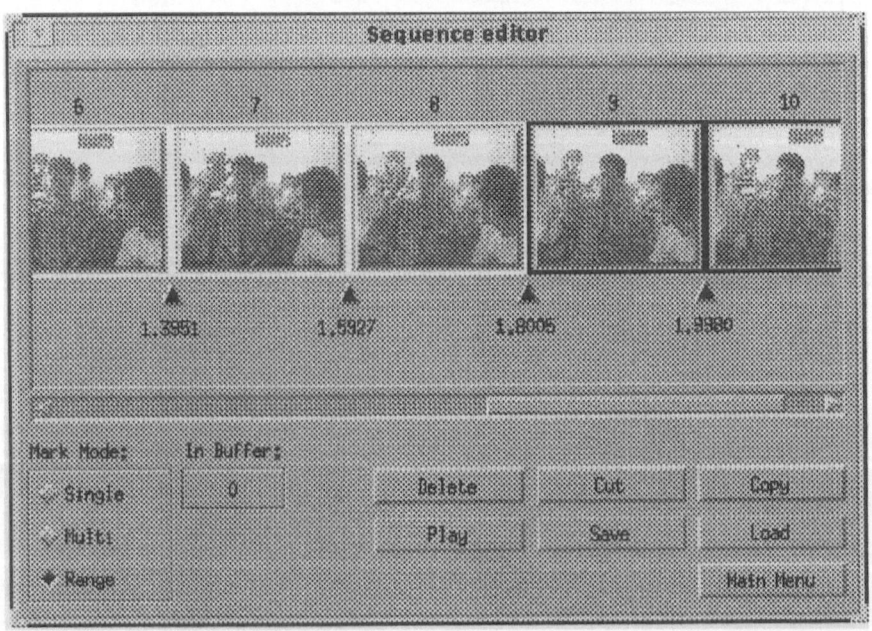

Fig. 5.15: An example of how a video chapter might look

The video editor has mainly two windows (record and play). In the record window the co-authors can enter the recording parameters before initiating the record of a sequence. The parameters are: time-recording (the user gives the time in seconds), frame-recording (the user gives the number of frames), stop-button (the user presses a button during the recording to stop it), resolution (360×287 or 180×143), speed: (As Fast As Possible or Frames/Second), grays: (16 or 128), compress: (On or Off), audio: (On or Off). In the play window the co-authors can watch a video sequence. The options are similar to those on a normal VCR (Slow back, Rewind, Play, Fast forward, Slow forward, Stop/Pause) and some playing parameters: frame number, play mode: Once or Loop, brightness.

During the simultaneous retrieval of multiple media streams (such as video and the corresponding audio) that constitute a video sequence, not only continuity of playback is maintained , but also the temporal relationships that existed among the media streams at the time of their recording are preserve are preserved. The different media streams constituting the video sequence may the recorded or processed by distinct processes/processors and may, hence, experience widely differing processing and transmission delays. This was taken care of by a mechanism that compares the display time of each frame with the time taken to record that frame. If the display time is too long then the next frame is skipped to avoid further delays.

5.4 Multimedia Communication

Among the several definitions for (a)synchronous communication, we have adopted the following: synchronous communication implies communication of the group members at the same time and asynchronous communication enables participants to communicate without implying communication of group members at the same time.

Synchronous communication is supported by means of audio, video and text channels, the WYSIWIS technique, the public comments, the co-author individual and global information. Synchronous communication allows the exchange of ideas about the editing task (discussing plans or concepts of the document, ways of drawing a mechanical part or writing a sentence) or about the document (discussing ideas or formats) and also about matters outside of the editing context (shall we play squash this evening?). We want to provide the advantages of both, so that a quick and user-friendly channel (video and audio) that is also non-ephemeral and safe (text) is provided.

Asynchronous communication is supported in the sense that co-authors can work independently of each other's presence in the editing session. The changes that the group members make in the document, both as document contents and as public comments, are examples of this. The CoMEdiA prototype tool provides the communication facilities on which to build the several

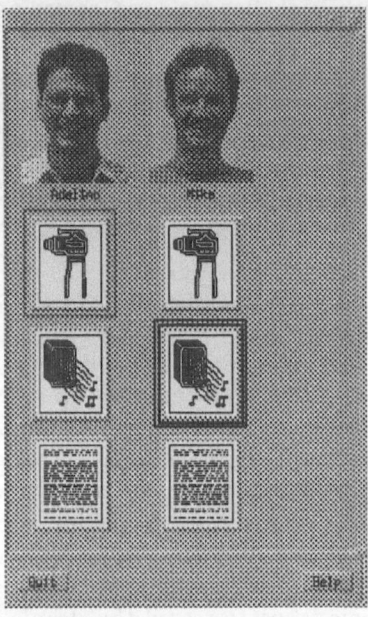

Fig. 5.16: The Channels window; it is used to establish a communication link (video, audio or text) between two co-authors

communication channels. It is easy for the co-authors to establish, use and close a communication channel (see Fig. 5.16).

5.4.1   Video Communication

Video communication has been technically possible for years, but at such great cost that it was not a realistic possibility for anyone but large organisations with especially designed network facilities for video-conferencing (Bellcore, NTT, Xerox, see [Galegher et at. 90a]). The use of standards and improvements in workstation technology have led to much smaller systems with lower costs. These developments have made video communication affordable to a wider range of smaller organisations.

By video communication we mean human communication by means of a continuous sequence of digital video images captured, transmitted and then displayed in order to support an adequate communication channel between co-authors. Digital video as a communication medium is a combination of several related software and hardware technologies for video capture, on-line video compression and decompression (CoDec), video transmission over a network and video display in a workstation window.

Fig. 5.17: Differences due to compression and decompression. The local image quality (left) is equivalent to the received image (right)

Video CoDec is one of the areas of technology currently receiving a great amount of attention. Because of high bandwidth required for video transmission, different compression algorithms were studied. Compliance with standards was an important aspect. MPEG (Motion Pictures Expert Group) is a standard for full motion video intraframe CoDec. Using a CoDec ratio of up to 100 this technique provides a high quality sequence of images, but is costly to encode and does not provide easy access to individual images of the sequence. JPEG (Joint Photographic Experts Group) is an industrial standard for still picture CoDec that achieves a CoDec ratio of up to 30. It is still costly, although less so than MPEG, but it can be implemented in software giving acceptable performances. If the JPEG standard is used for sequences of images it is called M-JPEG (Motion-JPEG).

Fig. 5.18: The video channel quality depending of the compression steps performed (DCT, quantisation and Huffman coding)

The video channel consists of a window to display the video images received from other co-authors with whom one has a video channel open. A

co-author can opt to receive its own video image that is exactly equal to the
one being transmitted. It may be that it is not equal to the one received
by the other co-author because of the information lost in the compression
and decompression algorithms. In Fig. 5.17 we show a local image (left) and
a received image (right). We have implemented an M-PEG algorithm (see
[Tritsch et al. 92]) for CoDec that provides the video channel with greyscale
images of resolution 176×144 pixels (Quarter Common Intermediate Format
- QCIF). The M-PEG algorithm can use 6, 10 or 15 compression coefficients.
Also, it is possible to vary the compression steps increasingly from no compression (see 5.17), using just the Discrete Cosine Transformation (see 5.18
left), the quantisation step (see 5.18 middle) and these plus the Huffman
coding (see 5.18 right). Finally it is possible to vary the number of greys
between 16 and 128.

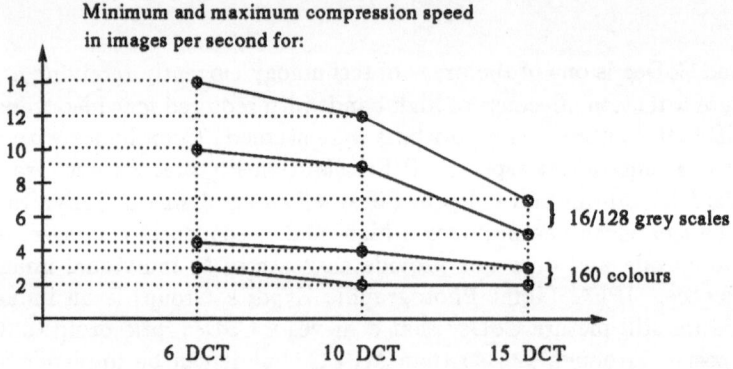

Fig. 5.19: CoDec speed in relation to image quality. Increasing quality
results in lower speeds

On Ethernet LAN, at a resolution of 176×144 and 16 greyscales per uncompressed image, we measured a peak video transmission rate of approx-
imately 80 images per second (see 5.19 and 5.20 and [Santos 93e]). Each
individual uncompressed image is ≈ 12 KB (16 greyscales) or ≈ 25 KB (128
greyscales) which results in a peak transmission rate of about 1 Mbyte/s.
Applying the CoDec algorithms, the image data size is dependent upon the
quality required. The CoDec rate of 20 to 30 (6 DCT coefficients) is the
fastest (10 to 14 images/s) but gives the lowest image quality. A medium
CoDec rate of 13 to 17 (10 DCT coefficients) gives 9 to 12 images/s with
medium quality. The CoDec rate of 9 to 12 (15 DCT coefficients) is the
slowest (5 to 7 images/s), but gives the highest quality. This applies for
both resolutions, 16 and 128 greyscales. Therefore, using a CoDec rate of 9
(≈ 2200 Byte/image) it would be possible to transmit about 500 images/s
using the same peak transmission rate. This shows that, with compressed

images, the LAN is not the limiting factor but the CoDec algorithms. We also measured performances using 160 colours' images of the same size. The CoDec rate of 7 to 10 (6 DCT coefficients) is the fastest (3 to 5 images/s) but gives the lowest image quality. A medium CoDec rate of 4 to 6 (10 DCT coefficients) gives 2 to 4 images/s with medium quality. The CoDec rate of 3 to 4 (15 DCT coefficients) is the slowest (2 to 3 images/s), but gives the highest quality.

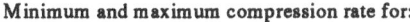

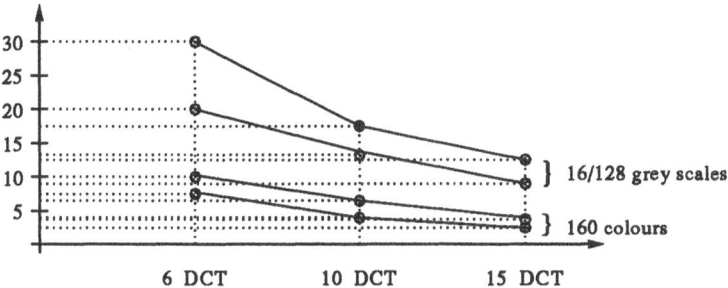

Fig. 5.20: CoDec rates in relation to image quality. A CoDec rate of 1:30 means that the original image data is reduced by a factor of 30

We have used the VideoPix (see Sect. 2.1.2) hardware-software solution for SUN workstations and the IndigoVideo (see Sect. 2.1.2) hardware-software tool for the Silicon Graphics workstations.

5.4.2 Audio Communication

Perhaps one of the most important components of any system for human-to-human communication is audio. In fact, most user complaints about teleconferencing are related to audio quality.

Different multimedia platforms provide different types of audio devices and services. Nevertheless, all of them offer a common set of functionalities, such as record, store and playback. Because of this general availability there are several audio formats depending on the platform. In CoMEdiA, we realised the audio channel considering the issue of cross-platform usability. The different audio formats considered were:

Sun workstations	SGI workstations	Multimedia PCs
U-LAW	AIFF	WAVE

We realised converters between these formats and used a subset of WAVE as intermediate format (see Fig. 5.21).

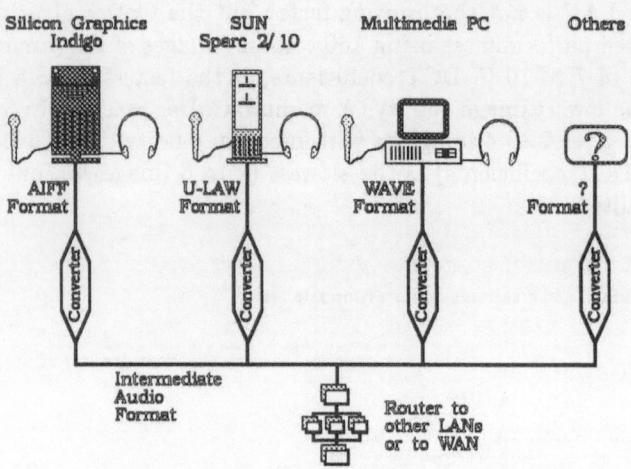

Fig. 5.21: The architecture of the audio communication in heterogeneous platforms. The data, in several formats, coming from/to the several devices is converted to/from a subset of the WAVE format

More than half the information transmitted during a tele-conference is verbal and therefore people notice when such an important information source is degraded. A major issue of the audio component is the sensitivity of the human ear with regard to timing errors. Here, the ear is significantly more sensitive than the eye. Delays and jitters within a certain time range ($\approx$ 50 to 200 milliseconds) that can be easily accepted with video sequences are unacceptable with audio sequences (see [Fish et al. 92]). Therefore, the audio channel plays a key role in a prototype system such as CoMEdiA, which aims at supporting co-authors' communication capacities.

In order to avoid overloading the network we introduced a noise gate. Only voice above a certain volume level is transmitted, but not the background noise during the time spans when no one is speaking or when the microphone is switched off. Audio does not require as much bandwidth as video. Because of this, we did not implement any compression algorithm. The audio channel has no particular user interface except the one used to connect or disconnect it.

5.4.3   Text Communication

Written communication allows non-ephemeral and safe communication concerning the editing task (discussing document plans or concepts or methods of drawing) or about the document (discussing ideas or formats) as well as matters outside the editing context.

The text channel is implemented using a window with an area to read messages from the other co-author and another to write.

5.4.4 Implicit Communication

In CoMEdiA co-authors can manipulate objects and see with no delay (except for the network delays) the manipulations done by other co-authors (WYSIWIS - see [Stefik et al. 87]). Thus, synchronous communication is provided by the editing *per se* (each co-author is aware of all the others). Other mechanisms that provide implicit communication have been referred in the previous sessions, namely individual information, global information, public comments and so on.

5.5 Algorithm and Architecture

Important results in groupware and CSCW have been achieved by improving existing solutions for distributed and networked systems. The basis of these solutions had been laid in distributed operating systems theory since the 80's (see [Lamport 78, Ricart et al. 81]). Groupware systems need parallelism control to resolve conflicts between participants' simultaneous operations. Groupware systems have been made possible by developing algorithms and architectures which support collaborative tasks. The main roles of these algorithms are to maintain a global coherence state of the cooperative system and to control the information flow amongst the co-users. By architecture we mean the way the cooperative system is organised in order to enable the cooperative algorithm to work. This organisation concerns the distribution of the physical processes and files over the different machines where the co-authors are located, as well as the way the communication is enabled. However, it has been shown that the requirements in these two fields are not exactly the same and so previous solutions are not completely acceptable for groupware systems. A basic conceptual difference is that distributed and database systems strive to give the user the illusion of being the system's only user, while groupware systems strive to make each user's actions visible and meaning clear to the others. Groupware presents a unique set of parallelism problems, and many of the approaches to handling parallelism in database applications and distributed systems - such as explicit locking or transaction processing - are not only inappropriate for groupware but can actually hinder tightly coupled teamwork. The important issues are:

Serialisation of co-authors' requests: the problem of deciding on the correct issuing order of the messages knowing that the transmission delay is random and unknown. The serialisation problem is common to any distributed system. CoMEdiA is distributed to allow geographically distinct processing, human cooperation and conferencing. Using CoMEdiA, co-authors processes compete for the access of an object through the server that manages the cooperation;

Mutual exclusion on the access: as cooperative processing assumes the existence of just one object available to several co-authors, most of the time the object (or parts of the object) has to be locked as critical. This means that accesses to these have to be made in a mutually exclusive manner. No two co-authors may edit the same picture or paragraph at the same time;

Global consistency of the document: after all network delays have been considered, the global state of the system (and of the multimedia documents) must be the same for all co-authors. This must be true independently of their geographic position relative to the server process or to other co-author process;

Responsiveness: interactions such as group brainstorming and editing are sometimes best carried out simultaneously. Synchronous systems supporting these activities should not hinder this cadence. To ensure this, two properties are required: a short response time or the time it takes for a user's own interface to reflect his or her own editing actions; and a short notification time, which is the time required for these actions to be propagated to everyone's interfaces;

Wide-area distribution: a primary benefit of groupware is that it allows people to work together, synchronously, even when separated by great physical distances. With communication technology, transmission times and rates for wide-area networks tend to be slower then for local area networks;, the possible impact on response time must therefore be considered. In addition, communication failures are more likely, pointing out the need for resilient parallelism control algorithms and architectures;

Data-replication: because a synchronous groupware prototype requires short response time, its data state may be replicated at each user's site. Many expensive operations can be performed locally. Consider, for instance, an editing session between a user in Darmstadt and another one in Amsterdam. If the users are working on a cooperative task with common windows, then if the objects (documents) being edited are not replicated, even scrolling or repairing a window overlap will require communication between the two sites - leading to a potentially catastrophic degradation of response.

Robustness: refers to the recovery from unusual circumstances, such as component failures or unpredictable user actions. Recovery from a site crash or a communication link breakdown is a familiar concern in distributed systems and groupware. Groupware must also be concerned with recovery from user actions. For example, adding a new user to a set of users issuing database transactions is not normally problematic, but adding a participant to an editing session can result in a major system reconfiguration. The cooperative algorithm must adapt to such a reconfiguration, recovering easily from such unexpected user actions as abrupt session entries or departures.

The differences between distributed systems solutions and groupware systems solutions occur in requirements concerning user response time, time and space distribution, data organisation, and user communication. One of the most problematic differences is that groupware deals with objects that we call "non-stable objects". In a conventional distributed system the objects exist and they are requested, used, freed and so on, without being destroyed (e.g. a printer or an XServer). Another particularity is that the object can be far away from the users. Usually in distributed systems the mutually exclusive objects are shared by variables or services that are physically located in each of the users. The co-authors processes negotiate the access but then the access itself is local. Also, the requests have to be memorised when they cannot be satisfied immediately. In the user and in the server there must be a memory mechanism associated with the algorithms.

5.5.1 The Possible Approaches and Analysis

There are two main classes of algorithms to support cooperation: **Client-Server** algorithms and **Order** algorithms (see [Santos 93f]). It is essential that the two classes of algorithms guarantee several properties, namely to synchronise the users' actions, ensure global consistency, prevent deadlocks, ensure mutual exclusion, and prevent starvation.

In the Client-Server algorithms there is a server process that is solely responsible for the management of the different properties referred above. The Clients are passive entities that transmit to the Server the information needed for this management (see [Greenberg et al. 92]). Usually the client processes run on different machines (each client process entails a user interface). The client processes do not communicate directly among them, and the server process keeps record of the system state.

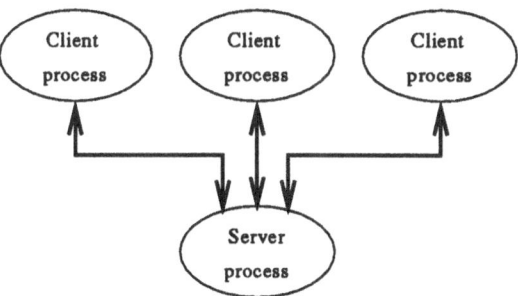

Fig. 5.22: The Client-Server's approach

In the Order algorithms there is no central entity to coordinate the actions, but rather each of the user processes must be "intelligent" enough to provide the management that was guaranteed before by the server process. One way of achieving this is the definition of time clocks and ordering events in the CME system to enforce a negotiation between the processes of each user to solve conflicts and establish synchronisation (see [Lamport 78]). Each client process has direct communication channels to all the other client processes and each client process keeps record of the system state which implies higher development complexity, run-time communication and management effort. In [Ricart et al. 81] Ricart presents an optimal algorithm for the synchronisation problems of this case.

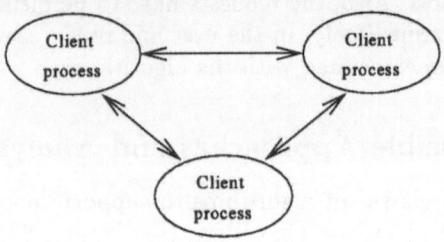

Fig. 5.23: The order algorithm's approach

There are three alternative architectures for groupware systems: centralised, replicated and hybrid. The **centralised** architecture consists of a single central process located on one machine, which controls the distributed work of all users, i.e. there is only one instance of the application program (see [Greenberg et al. 92]).

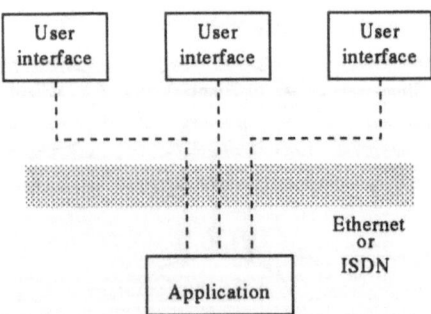

Fig. 5.24: Centralised architecture

Each user process is only responsible for channelling user input events to the central process (e.g. mouse movements, key inputs, window re-sizing) and for displaying the output sent by the central process. In fact, the user process does nothing more than terminal work. The central program processes the events sent by each user and notifies each one the output flow produced. It contains the run structures in their entirety and thus decides what to do with all the users' input/output. Therefore, this central program is frequently a large application.

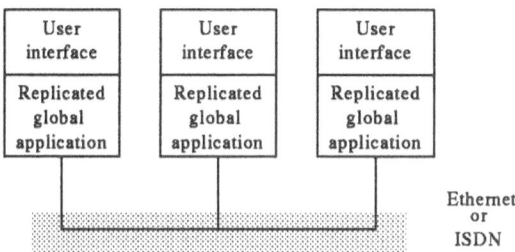

Fig. 5.25: Replicated architecture

The **replicated** architecture supports several application copies, one for each user, at each of the workplaces. There is no central process, and the replicated processes have to synchronise by communicating directly with each other. Each one is totally responsible for dealing with its local events, exchanging information with its counterparts on the network, and finally maintaining the integrity of its local run state. In order to support global coherence, each replicated application must also maintain the other users' run state locally. This allows correct repetition of their actions at each workplace. Generally, the run data structure is composed of a list, in which each entry reports to one user and holds his or her current run state.

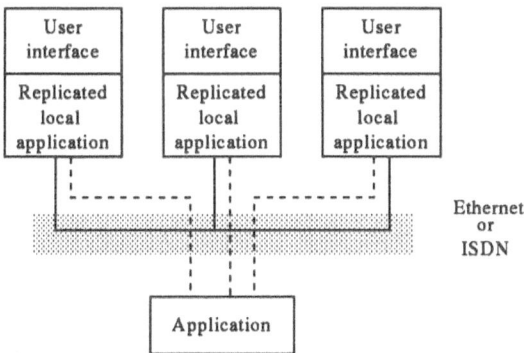

Fig. 5.26: Hybrid architecture

The **hybrid** alternative combines features of both the above. A variety of hybrid solutions are possible. They are commonly the ones adopted in concrete cases by combining the effectiveness qualities of the other two alternatives. Hybrid architectures have a central coordinating process that maintains the master copy of the internal representation, but each site as input, display and application representations as in the replicated architectures. The key difference is that input that could cause inconsistency (or possible conflicts between the user processes) is first sent to the co-ordinator process for approval, while operations guaranteed not to cause inconsistency are handled and displayed locally.

5.5.1.1   Analysis

It is easy to see that different architectures adapt better to different algorithms. For example, centralised architectures adapt better to Client-Server algorithms and replicated architectures to Order algorithms.

Centralised architectures have the advantage of hosting algorithms for which synchronisation and coherence maintenance are easy because all the information is located in one place. These architectures keep a consistent state across all views, since the input is serialised and only one copy of the internal structure exists. A disadvantage is that the complete system (all users) is vulnerable to failures of the server. However, in order for the results of manipulations to be displayed, the input must travel to the central site and back again, potentially allowing some "stickiness" (this is rarely a problem in LANs). Also, there is possible bottlenecking (network or processor) on the server because all activity must be channelled through it. The centralised approaches introduce the usual problems associated with centralised components (e.g. a single point of failure, a bottleneck).

Replicated architectures have the advantage of network traffic reduction because synchronisation and coherence information does not need to pass through a central agent and because only input-related data has to travel (which usually requires less bandwidth than display-related data). This reduces network traffic and bottlenecking and increases robustness. The response times are better, since the local displays are driven by the local copies of the applications. The disadvantage is the increased software complexity because of significant synchronisation problems.

An hybrid approach enables the response time to remain good, while input from the central co-ordinator process is broadcast to all the copies of the application; thus it also has lower bandwidth requirements than the centralised architecture. This also enables customisation of the local copy of the application. Finally, local processes can decide not only when to send input information to the central process, but also to which inputs they will react.

5.5.2 The Hybrid Algorithm of CoMEdiA

The cooperative algorithm used in CoMEdiA incorporates concepts from the two classes explained in Sect. 5.5.1. On the one hand, there is a *Global Server* process to perform the management. On the other hand, by means of the *Local Server* the user process gets more "intelligent", helping with the synchronisation problems. The algorithm used guarantees the properties referred to in Sect. 5.5.1. As the editing actions are performed by each of the co-authors they are transmitted to the *Global Server*, which re-transmits then to all the co-authors (including the one who originated it). There is no direct communication of editing actions between the users in the system. The *Global Server* receives and dispatches the users' requests using a FIFO rule. Therefore, this guarantees mutual exclusion and serialisation of the users' actions. There is no parallelism in the answer time (see [Marcos 92]).

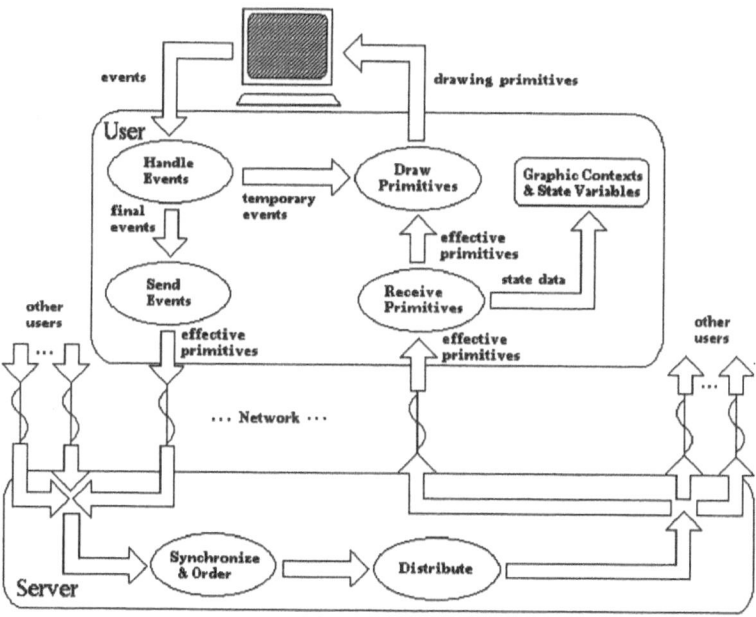

Fig. 5.27: The cooperative algorithm for the raster-images medium

By receiving the actions from the *Global Server* each user process executes them whether by changing the editing state variables (OtherUsersTable) or by outputting a result (see Fig. 5.27). The user actions are only definitively executed after receiving the *Global Server* answer (agreement). Furthermore, the WYSIWIS paradigm implies that even actions which are not directly connected with the visible editing but in any way affect the system state may not be executed without passing through the *Global Server* (changing the line pattern just has visible effects when the next line is drawn, but is transmitted as soon the user does it). The tendency is reflection of all editing actions. In this way, each user is complete aware of all editing states of the other users in the system, and the information unity is total.

The *Global Server* process is the only one with real access to the Multimedia Document being edited and each of the user processes has only a copy of the Multimedia Document. Precisely the maintenance of the coherency of these copies is the main goal of the algorithm.

5.5.3 The Hybrid Architecture of CoMEdiA

CoMEdiA implements a hybrid architecture. An external process (see the *Global Server* in Figs. 5.28 and 5.29) synchronises all the co-authors' actions and is also responsible for file system accesses. CoMEdiA is an XWindows based system, but does not use the X features to perform the distributed

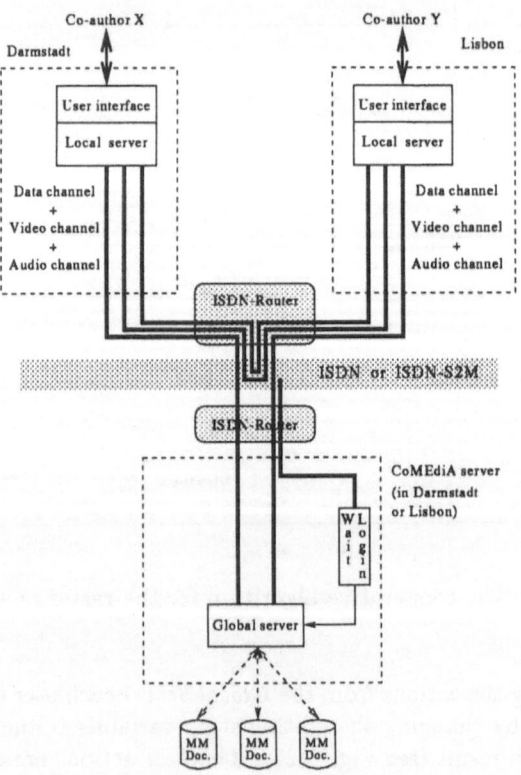

Fig. 5.28: An overview of CoMEdiA architecture (using ISDN-WAN)

processing. All the connections between the *Global Server* and the co-authors'
processes and between the co-authors' processes themselves are made using
Ethernet-LAN functions (TCP/IP) or ISDN-WAN.

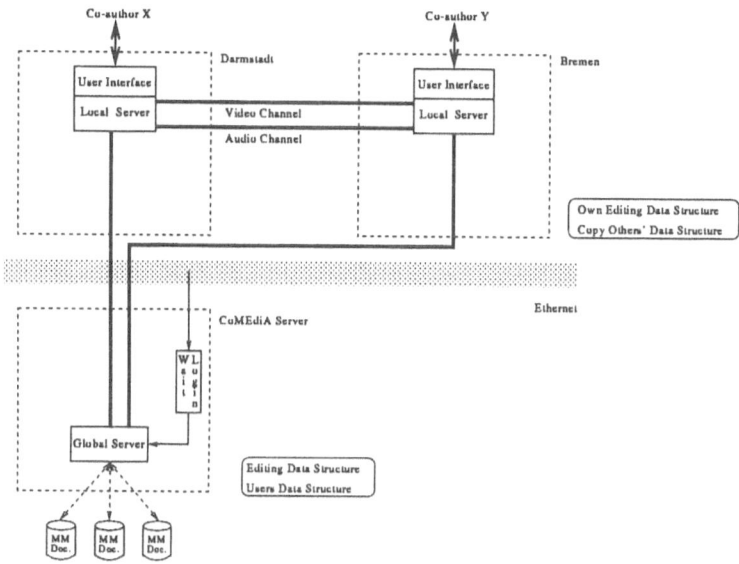

Fig. 5.29: A overview of CoMEdiA architecture (using an Ethernet-LAN)

Each user starts a process at his or her own workplace which establishes
a communication link with the *Global Server* (which is started automatically
if no link exists). After this connection is established the *Global Server* sends
all the information necessary for the new co-author process to register itself
has one more co-author in the editing session.

CoMEdiA as a multimedia and multi-user editing environment has several editors at any time, one for each active media. During a session, each
co-author process has its own editing state, depending on the individual's
manipulations, and needs to be aware of the other users' editing states to
repeat their actions properly on the local version (see [Marcos 92]). In the
Global Server structures only the information needed for total order aspects
of the system or disk accesses is stored.

5.5.4   Analysis of the Algorithm and Architecture of CoMEdiA

This algorithm is simple, not overloading the system (the message complexity
analysis reveals [2] messages per request). It has the disadvantage that co-
authors have to wait for their own input to be sent to the *Global server*, syn-

chronised, and returned, before they can see the result on their own screens. This makes the system less user-friendly. Nevertheless, this disadvantage can be overcome by simulating the input actions before sending them to the *Global server*.

The algorithm used to support cooperation in CoMEdiA guarantees mutual exclusion (just one co-author can access a document position or chunk at a time) and serialisation (if co-author X performs editing action x in the document before co-author Y performs action y then, independently of the network delays, action x will be effective before action y) in these accesses. It prevents deadlocks (every co-author process would be infinitely waiting for another co-author process to do something; no editing action by any co-author would ever be effective) and starvation (one co-author process would always be preempted in the accesses preventing its editing action from becoming effective) of any of the co-author processes, the fairness property (no co-author process has more priority than the others) is respected and the global consistency (the versions that the several co-authors see and process are coincident) of the document is maintained.

The architecture has the advantage of supporting a fairly simple cooperative algorithm. The *Global Server* enables the effective synchronisation mechanism to be implemented. Also, it is easy to establish a communication channel between co-authors. Nevertheless, it has the disadvantages common to any system with a centralised process through which all the information flows, namely those of fault tolerance and global delays.

We realise that the architecture of CoMEdiA is the most suitable for implementation in UNIX/X Windows environments because it separates the editing user interface tasks from the cooperation and coordination tasks. It enjoys the advantages of easily supporting an hybrid algorithm and having a simple network configuration (which can always be found where there are workstations connected by way of a LAN or a WAN). The algorithm realised within CoMEdiA is very simple to implement and ensures global consistency of the information copies, mutual exclusion in the accesses, serialisation of the user actions, and fairness in accessing the documents. It is almost totally implemented in a single physical process, which augments the robustness.

5.5.5 Different Hardware Platforms

We have limited our interest to workstations and microcomputers because they were the only feasible hardware solutions for our problem: low cost processing units for each group member, high communication availability and multimedia processing. Nevertheless, the conceptualisation made is completely independent of the platform and CoMEdiA has been implemented in a generic way so that it is as much independent of the platform as possible. This way, the following target platforms were considered:

- Workstation (UNIX, X-Windows) systems: CoMEdiA runs on SUN SPARCstation2, SUN SPARCstation10, SGI Indigo, DECstation 5000 with SunOS 4.1.x or Ultrix V4.3, X-Windows X11R5 and OSF/Motif 1.2.2. It does not require any kind of hardware or software extensions except the video grabber. It uses VideoPix in the SUNs, IndigoVideo in the SGIs (in the near future) and (also in the near future) MISTER COOL (see [Jäger 92]) in the PCs.

- Personal computer (MS-DOS, MS Windows) systems: realisation of a subset of the CoMEdiA prototype system in PCs with Microsoft Windows is currently underway. The subset entails the communication features, brainstorming, and text and raster images editing. The main difficulties lie in the fact that PCs (MS-DOS,MS Windows) are not pre-emptive multi-tasking and there are still problems in the inter-process communication (sockets and other known *de facto* standard communication strategies are still coming on the market in this platform).

We divide the CoMEdiA software into three parts to allow better explanation of the effort necessary when CoMEdiA is ported to other platforms:

- Editing and user interface (I): edit and cooperative algorithms implementation, as well as the interaction with the co-author;

- Network communication (II): communication over the network with remote machines and between the server and the user processes;

- Media devices handling (III): *drivers* for the audio and video devices using manufacturer-dependent libraries.

In the following considerations we did not account for difficulties that can arise from different processor types, colourmap policies, display hardware, memory constraints and so on, because they would occur whatever of the type of porting.

Workstations within the UNIX platform   If we had chosen another workstation manufacturer within the UNIX platform (IBM, HP, etc.) that used a UNIX-based operating system, X-Windows and OSF/Motif most of CoMEdiA would not have required changes. In (I) and (II) there would be no changes, because the mechanisms are all standard, being available independently of the manufacturer. In (III), changes would have to be programmed because the interfaces for dealing with the audio and video devices are not (yet) standard, so that they use manufacturer-dependent libraries.

Personal computers   If we had chosen the PCs/MS Windows platform the problems would be of a different nature. Within this platform there are no great differences between the manufacturers. Once the software runs on a machine using a certain MS Windows and MS-DOS version and using a given processor, then it will also run on any other machines from the same platform. This way, as mentioned above, in part (I) difficulties would appear in the non-preemptive multi-tasking nature of the platform. In (II) the problems could become more serious because the communication mechanisms are available from different vendors and there are occasional incompatibilities (an extra hardware peripheral board and access libraries have to be acquired). In (III) the interface to the media devices is different from the one of the workstations (although simpler), so new driver modules would have to be implemented.

Other platforms If we had chosen a completely different platform from the ones we have been working on (NeXT, Apple) the modifications would have to be more radical. The concepts and architecture of parts (I) and (II) could be still maintained, but hardly anything of the implementation. This happens because for both the NeXT and Apple platforms (these two here referred to as examples) the user interface and communication philosophies are comparable but the ways of implementing them are quite different from the UNIX platform. As an example, NeXT offers an "InterfaceBuilder" to allow a much more programmer-friendly implementation of user interfaces. The theoretical concepts behind it are not entirely new, but the way of expressing them is different. Concerning the network communication, NeXT has the concept of "Distributed Objects" that enables the sharing of distributed objects over a LAN, easing the programming of communication tools. In (III) the incompatibilities are complete and not even the concepts could be used, because this part of CoMEdiA is much more machine/platform-dependent.

Chapter 6

Applications and Usability Evaluation

> *"The key to understanding the group effectiveness problem is to be found in the on-going interaction process which takes place among group members."*

In this chapter we will deal with the practical applications of cooperative multimedia editing. We will describe the usability evaluation that was performed upon two case applications: cooperative software engineering and cooperative technical data production. We then analyse the data collected during the usability evaluation in order to obtain measurements and guidelines to feed into future versions of our prototype tool - CoMEdiA - or other future cooperative systems especially for multimedia processing.

The aims of this chapter are to provide the work with an accessible overview of usability evaluation and to show how evaluation methods can be used beneficially (see Sect. 6.2). There are five evaluation methods, namely the expert, the analytical, the observational, the survey and the controlled experiment method. All of these can have results depending on which view they reflect: expert, observer, designer and user view. The general differences among the five evaluation methods can be summarised under three main categories: the stage of prototype development for which they are suitable, the extent and type of user involvement and the production of qualitative, quantitative or diagnostic data.

In Sect. 6.3 we explain which evaluation strategies we take for CoMEdiA and the reasons for the decisions. We find that the best choices are an observational and a survey method.

In Sect. 6.4 we show the two case applications. The two case applications were chosen to cover the widest range of possible applications of the concepts, model and prototype implementation described in this work. We also formulate a set of experiment hypotheses to be checked by this usability study.

In Sect. 6.5 we analyse the data obtained by the two methods. In Sect. 6.6 we compare the CoMEdiA prototype, with other similar systems described in Sect. 2.4. The comparison is quantitative and is based on what was explained in Sects. 3.2 and 4.5. The goal is to build a table relating the technology-level input factors with group benefits.

Improvements in computer technology and tele-communication have made possible a new class of application systems intended to support group work. The objective of these systems is to support editing, meetings, coordination, project management, decision making on a variety of activities. However, the evaluation of these systems presents a unique set of new problems. Evaluating software for support of group work and multimedia has two components. The first component involves the normal criteria and methods applied to the evaluation of any application software product. The second component addresses those issues that are unique to group work.

We define the usability of a prototype system as the degree to which specific users can achieve specified goals in a particular environment with effectiveness, efficiency and satisfaction. Usability evaluation matters to everyone who has to do with information technology, and people are increasingly aware of its significance. Usability reflects all those aspects about a system which enable people to make use of the system effectively, efficiently, and with satisfaction and to perform their work tasks. It is affected by factors ranging from detailed design decisions about screen layout to the broadest organisational issues. The importance of usability evaluation has grown with the spread of computers into almost every area of our lives (not every computer user is a computer expert). At the same time, information technology developers increasingly wish to learn more about how to build a high level of usability into systems. Many of the answers are being found in the Human-Computer Interaction (HCI) domain, by professionals and researchers with diverse backgrounds such as human factors, computer science and ergonomics.

To succeed in developing systems which meet the needs of the user and provide an acceptable level of usability, we need some means of assessing just how well a system meets those aims. To be reliable and cost-effective, the process of evaluation must use suitable methods. We also need evaluation methods that help us diagnose just what is wrong with a design or identify specific factors that make it difficult to use, so that the system can be improved.

6.1 Evaluation Rationale

Evaluating software designer to support group work and multimedia has two components. The first component involves the normal criteria and methods applied to the evaluation of any application software product. The second component addresses those issues that are unique to group work. Normal criteria applied to (single-user) software include such factors as:

- Functionality: what features does the product have and how well do they match the work task to be performed?

- Integration: how well are the components of the product related to each other?

- Interface: how well has the user interface been designed and how does it match the intended user population in the work setting?

- Support: how much training and technical assistance will be needed by the intended user population?

- Reliability: how well is the product coded, what type of developer support is likely to be needed, will the product be enhanced, and will the developer firm survive?

- Efficiency: what resources are needed to run the product and how well does the product fit in with other products in the user's immediate operating environment?

- Ease of modification: what can be changed and how easily?

- Economics: what are the costs of using the product and how do they compare with the anticipated benefits?

Usability is the one software quality most constantly apparent to the end-user of a system. When we come to make serious use of a product, its usability for the tasks we wish to perform is central in shaping our opinion. It can concern performance, beauty or realism of the output, reaction speed or user friendliness. If the product fails to help us to perform our tasks efficiently, effectively and with satisfaction, then we will be likely to form a poor opinion of it. The history of information technology is littered with products with poor usability. This incurs costs for the user in terms of training time, work quality, satisfaction; costs for the producer in terms of demands for software support and future losses of sales.

Such failures can be avoided by evaluating usability and learning from previous results. By incorporating appropriate methods for usability evaluation into system development, producers can assess usability at the development of stages and so improve the quality of their software. The two main objectives of an evaluation process can be identified as:

- To determine the effectiveness or potential effectiveness of a prototype system in its several aspects (user interface, performance, group support, and so on);

- To provide a means of suggesting improvements.

Evaluation must provide diagnostic information if its results are to be used to improve a system: data that help identify specific areas for improvement and data that point to those elements in the design and in the implementation that are causing problems. It must provide information that can be quickly fed back into development. Qualitative evaluation of performance will involve judgements about what is done easily or with difficulty and attempted diagnosis of usability defects and their causes. Qualitative data focus on reports and opinions that may be categorised in some way but not reduced to numerical values. The evaluation can also be quantitative, involving timing and measurement of task performance. Quantitative data deal with either user performance or attitudes recorded in numerical form.

6.2 Usability Evaluation Strategies

Anyone trying to find the most suitable way of evaluating the usability of a specific system will want answers to questions about alternative methods, different benefits and resources required, the appropriate timings within the system development cycle, the expected results, and the possible analyses of the results. Mainly, the choice of the evaluation method depends upon the purpose of the evaluation, the resources available and the cost. These are the issues we will approach in this Sect..

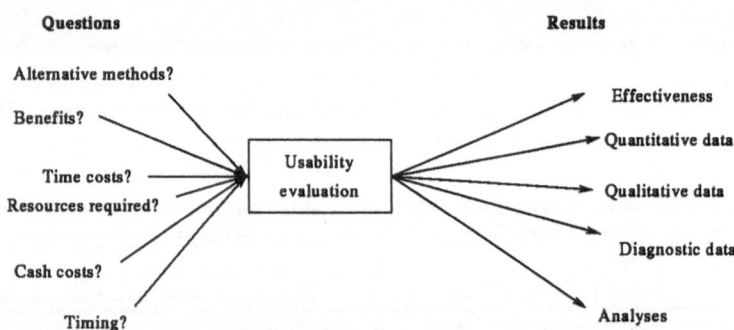

Fig. 6.1: Possible questions in the search for a suitable way to evaluate the usability of a system

It is a known fact that people perceive things differently, and that judgements made from one viewpoint may not match judgements made from another. If an evaluation is subjective, we need to know whose view it reflects before we can judge the worth of the evaluation. For evaluation results to be valid, the evaluation must tell us about the usability of a system for its intended end-user. This lies at the very heart of the user-centred design and evaluation. Therefore, there are several possibilities for assessment of the evaluation, depending on the viewpoints.

The designer's view Designers, not unnaturally, tend to find their own systems easy to use. They typically have a high level of expertise with a system, and well-developed knowledge of the underlying details of implementation that define precisely the way a system works. Such practised familiarity can make it difficult to anticipate the kinds of problems other users will encounter. In fact, without some training in evaluation methods it is far from simple for a designer to judge how easily an end-user will be able to perform a task. The designer must be fully briefed about the expected levels of skill possessed by the intended users and about specific tasks that will be typical of the actual work the intended user will be performing.

The expert's view HCI professionals and others who perform expert evaluations face some of the same problems. They have the advantage of knowing a lot about what end-users can and cannot do easily. But their own expertise and knowledge will not match the expertise and knowledge of the intended end-user. Experts have to make judgements, predictions and educated guesses about usability for other people, based on their own use or study of the system. They should take into consideration the anticipated skills and the knowledge of the user, the work tasks the user will perform, and the intended work context. Generally, some training or guidance is advantageous when non-specialists seek to produce this kind of evaluation. Recent work suggests that a small amount of training can be highly cost-effective in enabling non-specialists to perform evaluations.

A more objective view So far, we have reviewed methods that do not really involve the end-user in the evaluation process. If a system or prototype is available then there is no substitute for getting real, representative end-users to try it out, and observing or measuring how well they get on (this is why these are also known as observational methods). This can give a much more accurate picture of usability. It allows the evaluator to measure how usable a system really is, in the hands of the people for whom it is designed. At their simplest, such evaluations should involve observing intended users performing sample tasks with the prototype system. The circumstances in which the observation is carried out should match the intended normal working environment as closely as possible.

A more precise record of the way in which the end-user interacts with the system while performing a task can be captured on video. This can be done in a usability laboratory or in an actual working setting; in either case, it is important that the users should find the process of recording inconspicuous and that it does not interfere with their work. Analysis of a detailed video recording of task performance can provide considerable insight into how well, and how easily, users perform specific operations and tasks when using the system. It also allows the derivation of quantitative information about the usability of the system.

The user's view Methods in which the user's view is determinant are also known as survey methods. What users think about a system when they use it is a primary factor in determining its usability. Surveying the subjective opinions of the end-users can be used as an evaluation technique in its own right, or it can provide rich additional information for observational performance based evaluations. Some cautions is needed concerning the manner of collecting subjective information, particularly verbal data. If users are asked to describe what they are doing while they do it, this may change the way they perform their task. If they are asked to report some time afterwards, they may miss, or misrepresent, important factors. Methodical collection and interpretation of subjective data allows the evaluator to build up a composite picture of the system's usability from the end-user's viewpoint.

The cheapest and quickest evaluation method will often be to employ someone with expertise in usability to produce a specialist report: an **Expert Method**. This can give a lot of information very quickly, can diagnose significant faults, and provide specific recommendations. However, much depends upon the quality of the expertise. There can also be difficulties in feeding the results back into design and implementation phases.

Where the priority is to perform usability evaluation early in the design phase, an **Analytic Method**, although narrow in scope, can give very early feedback.

For a more broadly revealing picture of usability, it is advisable to evaluate with real end-users, performing representative tasks, in a real or simulated work setting,.e. to employ user-based methods. Objective usability data can be gained by observing users and analysing how well they perform their tasks: an **Observational Method**. This can give both diagnostic and quantitative information about usability. For thorough observational evaluation it may be best to use the services of a professional usability centre or laboratory, although it is possible to achieve good results in-house. For the most effective communication of results back to the design team, designers should have an active involvement in the evaluation process, and see for themselves. Where users are prepared to participate actively in such a method, and to explain why they do things and what is difficult, then the method can be quite effective.

The cheapest way of eliciting a lot of information directly from users is to use a questionnaire: a **Survey Method**. It is preferable to use a questionnaire that has been scientifically developed for the purpose. Such questionnaires should give trustworthy quantitative data about different aspects of usability, when completed by ten or more users. Questionnaires can also be tailored to elicit diagnostic information about a particular system; in such cases it requires some expertise to interpret the resulting data.

Formal **Controlled Experimental Studies** is another method that tends to be very costly and complex. Usually, there are so many potentially relevant variables in the characteristics of the users (the tasks they perform, and the technical physical and organisational environments in which the system is to be used) that there are considerable difficulties in generalising from the findings of such a study.

6.2.1 Observational Method

This method involves *real users* using *working systems*. Observational methods can range from almost entirely informal to highly structured: in essence, users are observed interacting with a system. Often their interaction is recorded in some way for later observation and analysis. To be helpful in evaluating the usability of the system, even the most informal approach to observation requires that the user has some tasks to perform with the system. Observational methods offer extra benefits when designers and decision makers also take part in the observation. Designers of a system that has usability flaws may be more easily persuaded of the facts when they see it with their own eyes. Managers comparing possible alternative systems or considering a system for acceptance get an opportunity to see how usable it can be.

The simplest way of applying this method is for someone familiar with usability issues to observe users performing tasks with the system. If the system is fully implemented and in its natural work setting, then simple observation can tell us much about the use and usability of the system in that setting. Unfortunately, knowledge of being observed can be intrusive, and can affect the way work is performed. This way of observational method is somewhat "hit and miss": any detail which the observer may overlook is irretrievably lost. Observers have to analyse at the same time as they observe.

Simple observation of users can give useful insights, and is especially valuable when used in conjunction with other evaluation methods, such as interviews. In short we can say that it: Requires a prototype system ready for use; Is user-based and involves user performance of work tasks; Is relatively simple to execute; Requires an expert observer to extract maximum relevant information; Can take place in a work setting; May interfere with what is being observed.

Making a video record of the interaction between user and system offers real advantages. It also incurs additional cost: in facilities required and in time to analyse the data. Some people may feel uneasy about "being watched", and it is essential that recordings are made only with the informed consent of the users being filmed. Most video recording and analysis takes place in usability laboratories, although an in-house solution is also possible. By using different cameras, it becomes possible to capture and synchronise data about the user behaviour. A major cost has been the time required to analyse the data: cases of up to 10 hours to analyse one single hour of recording have been registered.

With this technique, data capture can be separated from analyses. These two elements of evaluation can be performed in different locations and at different times. This also enables the involvement of managers, designers and future users in the evaluation, by giving them roles or simply inviting them into the viewing sessions. Their committed involvement can greatly assist in the shaping of the final system. Equally important, it can help the future end-users to feel that the system has been designed with their needs in mind. In short we can say that this method: Requires a prototype system ready for use; Is user-based and involves user performance of work tasks; Creates a revisable record of the interaction; Allows detailed analysis of interaction data; Can be time-consuming to analyse; Can be exploited to bring together managers, designers and end-users.

The idea of automated, effortless gathering of data about how people use systems (automating the collection of objective, accurate data about interaction) is very appealing. Software logging methods usually just require work modifying the software to include the collection of data. The principle of recording some kind of interaction log is well established. Collections of logs can be analysed statistically, to show the frequencies of use of different commands. A log can be analysed to reveal errors or inappropriate commands.

Graphical user interfaces present different problems for the collection and analyses of a log. The user is interacting directly with objects such as buttons, scroll bars, microphones or video cameras. The system is responding in subtle ways - for example capturing one more video frame - as well as executing commands. If all the user and system actions occurring over a period of time are recorded, at a fine level of detail, then so much data may be collected that analyses become very difficult.

This technique requires that the prototype system is especially programmed to record certain user and system actions, and to allow the evaluator access to this record. The key is which actions should be recorded. Too much data, especially to much low-level data, makes the analyses difficult. In short we can say that software logging: Requires a prototype system ready for use; Is user-based and involves user performance of work tasks; Provides easy and inexpensive collection of data; Is usually unobtrusive; Can give a detailed time-stamped record of the interaction; Can be facilitated by specific software tools for monitoring and analyses; Generates data which can be difficult to analyse.

Verbal protocols are records of users' spoken observations and thoughts. Video recording is coupled with some form of verbal record, known as a verbal (or think aloud) protocol, produced by a user while undertaking the tasks. The protocol can yield a wide range of information, for example, the user's planning for the particular task, recall of commands and arguments, understanding of the operations, and system responses and error situations. However, users often find it difficult to put their thoughts in words while trying to solve a problem. Variations on verbal protocols include evaluating the performance of pairs of users, incorporating question-asking, or obtaining protocols after the tasks have been completed (post-event protocols). In the case of post-event protocols users view videos of their actions and provide a commentary on what they were trying to do. An obvious advantage of this variation is that it is suitable for use with tasks that are safety-critical, require intense concentration or are time-critical.

Interactive observation is a variant on straightforward observational evaluation. The main feature is that there is a hidden operator who either simulates all the output from the system or amends user input and system output to overcome deficiencies in the system.

6.2.2   Survey Method

Survey methods give the evaluator access to the user's subjective views of a system. They involve *real users*, but information is not gathered while the users are interacting with the system.

Questionnaires give a very cost-effective access to data about the usability of a system. They offer the real advantage of providing data about the end-user's views of system quality, rather than some expert or theoretician's view, and can provide data about system usability in a real work setting. However, the data gathered may vary in quality. *Closed questions* can constrain answers to yes/no, or to a point on a scale of preference. They require careful construction to avoid ambiguity and to gather data of the required scope about the system and its use. *Open questions* allow the expression of relevant criticism, but can be difficult to analyse. It is widely accepted that clearly focused questions are the most likely to yield useful information.

The simplest rating scales are checklists consisting of basic alternative responses to a very specific question. For example, a three-point scale 'yes', 'no', don't know' is often used. Checklists are also used to check the presence or absence of particular features. More complex multi-point scales increase the number of points in the rating scales; the meanings of either each individual point or just the end points are given. A popular form of attitude scale used in HCI research is the semantic differential scale. This scale has opposite adjectives (as easy-difficult, or clear-confusing) at the end points, and respondents rate on a scale between these paired adjectives. Finally, a named scale can be dispensed with and particular items can be placed in a specified numerical order. For example, items can be ranked for their usefulness. A rank ordering process is most successful for limited groups of items, as large groups can mean that responders give arbitrary rankings. In short we can say that the questionnaire method: Requires a prototype system ready for use; Is user-based and involves user performance of work tasks; Can be highly cost-effective; Can yield subjective views about use of system in work context; Can constrain the nature of data gathered (by asking some questions, but not others); Can only gather retrospective views.

Interviews are much more time consuming than questionnaires, if a large sample of users is to be included in the survey. They require careful pre-planning, and a good degree of expertise in the interviewer, to ensure that the questions cover all the relevant topics and are not delivered in a way that unduly influences the nature of the reply. A structured interview, with a predetermined set of precisely phrased questions, is required if data are to be analysed statistically.

A flexible interview, covering pre-specified topics but in a style and order shaped by the responses of the user, can elicit revealing points, and it allows interviewers to pursue interesting lines of inquiry. Results may be more difficult to analyse en masse, but individually they can be highly informative. Some people choose to record interviews, whose analyses can be time-consuming. In short we can say that the interview method: Requires a prototype system ready for use Is user-based and involves user performance of work tasks Can elicit helpful information about users' views

6.3   Evaluation Strategy for CoMEdiA

The Fig. 6.2 presents the key characteristics of each of the five methods referred above, summarising their main advantages and disadvantages. The general differences among the five evaluation methods can be summarised under three main categories: the stage of prototype development for which they are suitable, the extent and type of user involvement and the production of qualitative, quantitative or diagnostic data (the three first rows on table in Fig. 6.2).

Criteria/Method	Analytic	Expert	Observational	Survey	Experiment
Timing of use	early	any	late	late	any
User-based	no	no	yes	yes	yes
Quantitative data	yes	no	yes	yes	yes
Qualitative data	no	yes	yes	yes	yes
Diagnostic data	narrow	yes	yes	yes	narrow
Scope	narrow	broad	broad	broad	narrow
Expertise	high	high	mean	mean	high
In-house	no	possible	yes	yes	no
Time costs	mean	low	mean	low/mean	high
Cash costs	low/mean	low	mean	low/mean	high
Advantages	timing; costs	costs; diagnostic; scope; quick	user; diagnostic; scope	user; diagnostic; scope; quick;	user; rigorous
Disadvantages	scope; non-user	non-user; not reliable	timing;	timing;	scope; costs

Fig. 6.2: Key characteristics to help in the choice of one of the five evaluation methods.

In our specific case we want to evaluate the usability of the cooperative multimedia editing prototype system CoMEdiA. It is already a ready-to-use prototype system whose usability we want to test with real users (user-based evaluation) in a real work environment (late evaluation). We do not have a high expertise in evaluation, and from a cost point of view we cannot employ an expert to proceed with the evaluation. We need to be able to do it in-house with low or moderate costs.

We evaluate how well the application system functionalities work. For example, how well the system supports individual tasks. This is similar to evaluating a normal single-user prototype system where one is concerned with the features supported, the degree of the integration of these features, and the quality of the interface. Performance also refers to how well the system supports those activities that are unique to group work, for example, group decision making, exchanging public comments or having a multimedia communication channel open. We also evaluated the features provided by the application to support communication, for example whether one can reply to textual message or whether one can refuse or accept a new communication channel. It was also necessary to know how well the system keeps track of the resources available, assigned and used; how easy it is to enter this information; how easy it is to obtain it; and how status is determined. We find that the best choices from the previous five are the **observational** and the **survey** methods.

For a comprehensive evaluation of usability, it is sensible to use more than one method. In light of this and of the factors explained above we employed the combination of an observational method to evaluate user performance and a survey method to evaluate user satisfaction. We also need a method aimed at measuring and reporting properties of a completed system. It must help us to identify the causes for any shortcomings and it must produce a set of usability measurements and guidelines. Concerning what has been said in Sect. 6.2 we would like to take an objective and a user view.

6.3.1 Observational Method

From the five procedures of the observational method we use software logging. We introduced changes to CoMEdiA in order to gather data about its use.

6.3.1.1 Network Performance

Here we intended to determine the performance of the different network types over which CoMEdiA runs (Ethernet LAN, Internet WAN and ISDN WAN). We implemented measuring routines to enable us to know the amount of Kbps a network allows CoMEdiA to transfer. During several days we measured the performance of these networks while CoMEdiA was running. The Figs. below represent values taken at several time spots over several hours during the day.

Ethernet LAN: offers the best performance, as expected. The nominal rate of these networks is 10 Mbps, although the effective rate should not be less than 1 Mbps. The transmission times are rather constant (light line), and the transmission rate grows with the size of the messages. This shows that the network tries to respond to more network load with more bandwidth. The effective rate is between 1 Mbps and 5 Mbps.

Internet WAN: is a packet-oriented network and as such has unpredictable performances (depending on the network load of the moment). The transmission rate and transmission time grow with the size of the messages. This also shows that the network tries to respond to more network load with more bandwidth. The effective rate is between 2 Kbps and 12 Kbps (much inferior to Ethernet).

ISDN WAN: is a circuit-switched network and therefore should have constant transmission rate. As expected the transmission rate is rather constant (44 Kbps). The 64 Kbps rate that the ISDN connection supplies is not reached, because we used a router and a terminal adapter to bridge from the LAN to the ISDN. This introduces overhead from the conversion and routing of the packets, and from the use of a piece of the LAN (between the machines and the routers). This would be avoided if we had re-programmed the communication layer of CoMEdiA to use ISDN directly.

6.3.1.2 Editing Performance

Here we measured network occupancy and processing load during one editing session of CoMEdiA. As control point we used the messages transmitted between the server and each of the user processes. The parameters measured were the number and frequency of the messages, their type, size and time required to perform the editing operations. The recorded session lasted for about 15 minutes. The minimum size of the messages is 12 Bytes. In the text medium editing, the message SEND_NEW_CA1_TG (a comment or annotation has been created) needs 215 Bytes to transmit the comment. On the other hand, the messages LITTLE_CHAR (a new character has been typed by one co-author) and CHANGED_CURSOR (the cursor position has been changed by on co-author) have a high occurrence index but on average take almost minimal information. In the raster images medium, the PIX_LINE (free-hand functionality) was the most frequently sent message. In the three examples, WANT_MEDIUM_ID (a new chapter is going to be created), OPEN_FILE (a document file is opened) or CLOSE_FILE (a document file is closed) are examples of requests that are used very seldom. These measures helped us to set some implementation parameters (such as the size of the messages to transmit) and yielded information on which requests should be optimised for speed and which for size.

6.3.2 Survey Method

From the two procedures of the survey method, we selected questionnaires. These were presented to the subjects at the end of the experiments. Most of the statements showed a positive attitude to CoMEdiA; others were negative, which helped to reveal spots for improvement. Moreover, we present our own experience gathered from our own use, as well as the knowledge acquired from informal talks with other users.

6.4 Two Case Applications

In Fig. 6.3 we give a classification of the CoMEdiA features in the field of the several approaches to computer-supported cooperative work presented in Sect. 2.3.1. Three points mean that CoMEdiA is thought to have features that will allow good support for the approach, and zero points means that CoMEdiA has no features that would support the approach.

Face-to-face meetings		
1	Group decision support systems	1
5	Computer-supported face-to-face meetings	1
Remote meetings		
4	Group authoring and editing software	3
6	Screen-sharing software	2
7	Computer conferencing software	2
8	Information-filtering software	0
9	Computer-supported video tele-conferences	2
13	Non-human "participants" in group meetings	0
Activities between meetings		
2	Project management software	0
3	Calendar management for groups	1
10	Conversational structuring	0
11	Computer-supported spontaneous interaction	1
12	Comprehensive work group support: Multimedia	3

Fig. 6.3: CoMEdiA's coverage diagram (0 - not supported, 3 - good support)

Although the focus of the evaluation is on the group work, at the most primitive level most work is performed by individuals and a major portion of the evaluation process is performed by individuals. Consequently, a major portion of the evaluation process for a group support application product must consider how well that product supports an individual performing.

We will evaluate real applications of the prototype system CoMEdiA, namely:

- Cooperative software engineering

- Cooperative technical data production (Technical report production and budget calculation)

The observations were conducted in laboratory conditions, i.e. the groups were brought together in order to be subjects of the experiments and they would not have performed the task otherwise. The logging files were collected during the experiments (e.g. all the actions and communication were recorded) and then backed up for later analysis, and the questionnaires were answered right after the experiments. There were follow-up informal talks with the subjects to catch subjective non-explicitly expressed opinions.

6.4.1   Cooperative Software Engineering

In order to be able to test CoMEdiA for cooperative software engineering, we built a tool on top of the CoMEdiA architecture called Cooperative Programming Tool (CPT). CPT is a system that enables several users (programmers) connected by a network to work together in order to develop software. This work can involve cooperation among analysts, developers and programmers as well as the participation of experts who can occasionally be asked to take part in the development. The cooperative software development process involves activities such as conceptualisation, design and specification, editing, integration of software components (units or modules), debug, test and automatic generation of reports.

The tool has an interface similar to that of CoMEdiA. For editing, only the text medium is necessary. For the conceptualisation and development phase we kept the brainstorming tool. The communication channels are as in CoMEdiA (video, audio and text), and the several mechanisms of multi-user interface and awareness were also maintained. New capabilities were added to enable the use of standard compiling ("cc" and "gcc") and debugging ("dbx") tools. The editing of modules, compiling, debugging and testing are done cooperatively, all the users having the option of becoming active (giving input and receiving output).

The test was performed by a group of programmers who use CPT to conceive, implement, test and demonstrate a software program. The participants already knew each other, and some of them had even already worked together. All the participants had computer interaction experience.

The group was asked to produce a program that asks about and compares the weather in the workplaces where the several programmers are working and to compile a table with them and some additional comments. One key aspect was the negotiation necessary to decide about the program data structures and about the presentation of the table. They had 30 minutes available to fulfil this task and were working in a non-face-to-face situation.

6.4.2   Cooperative Technical Data Production

The test was performed by a group of people who work in a travel agency and had to prepare a multimedia holiday offer and budget using CoMEdiA. The participants already knew each other, and some of them had even already worked together. All the participants had computer interaction experience.

For this test we used CoMEdiA as it is, without the special-purpose tool on top. In order to prepare the multimedia holiday offer and budget, the group was given a video sequence of a holiday destination and a description of the local tourist attractions. The group was asked to produce a multimedia document with at least three components: a small text describing the offer (a quarter of a page), a chart with the budget and a video sequence (based on the initial one) with the local attractions. One key aspect was that the group had to negotiate the presentation of the tourist information. Also, each member of the group has different information and experiences to contribute, as well as having different skills. They had 30 minutes available to fulfil this task and were working in a non-face-to-face situation.

6.4.3   Experimental Hypotheses

Following the ideas explained in Chaps. 3 and 4, we wanted to test the concepts developed. In this way, we formulated a set of experiment hypotheses to be checked by this usability study.

H.1 Multiple-cursors, tele-pointing, gesturing and WYSIWIS support good co-author awareness and help the progress of the cooperative process.

H.2 Consistency of the overall work and constant validation are eased.

H.3 The support given for brainstorm activities, both in the brainstorming area and in the multimedia communication channels, is good enough for the conceptualisation necessary to perform the task.

H.4 Mechanisms for annotation (private) and commenting (public) are useful.

H.5 The information generated and made available about other co-authors is adequate and useful.

H.6 The multimedia communication channels are helpful, and an audio channel is more important and useful than a video channel.

H.7 Non-face-to-face groups have access to better available expertise and possibly to richer information and technological environments.

H.8 In non-face-to-face meetings there is less opportunity to "socialise" and participants get down to the matter in hand more quickly.

H.9 Uninhibited behaviour occurs more frequently via multimedia channels than in face-to-face communication, and the amount of simultaneous speech and the time between different speakers are reduced.

H.10 Multimedia channels are suited to informal communication, especially to aiding the uncertain and equivocal aspects of communication.

H.11 Concurrent access to information and non-awareness of the information's physical location are plus points.

H.12 Consensus is more difficult to reach than in a face-to-face situation.

6.5   Analysis of the Results

In general terms, the experiments were successful, demonstrating the usability and usefulness of the CoMEdiA prototype system. Moreover, demonstrations of the prototype were very frequent during the implementation, which continues to be the case.

The editing sessions and demonstrations usually run without problems, although once in a while the prototype crashes (as with almost any research prototype). There were hardly any problems attributable to the heterogeneity of the platforms used. This demonstrates the viability of applications suitable for running on different hardware platforms. Crashes due to a network failure were very rare. This demonstrates that an application can successfully run in different networks (Ethernet, Internet and ISDN).

The subjects expressed enthusiasm for the technology and prototype system used. They reported that they felt comfortable with it, found it easy and natural to use overall, and a means to good editing work and communication. The editing media available were said to be expressive enough. Some subjects reported the usefulness of integrating the computer-generated animations medium. There were mixed answers concerning their performance as individuals and the performance of the group. There was both overall satisfaction and specific frustration with the quality of the document created. Comparing the test with a face-to-face situation, they considered they had produced an output in less time and with better quality, but there were mixed opinions about whether there had been less stress (perhaps due to the technology) or more user satisfaction. Apart from the graphical output quality, they reported satisfaction with the results obtained. They expressed frustration when drawing with the mouse. A stylus would have been better.

In the end, the subjects were aware of the changes in the working style they undertook, and they felt they had contributed equally to the discussion and the final product. Also, given the choice they would not have chosen to work alone on the same kind of task.

Subjects agreed that CoMEdiA was easy to learn and work with. This can be attributed to the analogy of many of the mechanisms used in CoMEdiA to the typical paper-and-pen situation, to the problem-oriented approach (instead of a task-oriented one), and to the simple syntax.

There was a overall positive evaluation of the communication, co-author awareness, tele-presence, and gesturing mechanisms. Still, the quality of presence was inferior to that in a face-to-face situation. For example, we observed two occasions when visually separated but co-located participants involved in an intense discussion left their computers to speak face-to-face.

There is a strong focus of attention on the work surface. Subjects' eyes remained fixed to the editing area for long periods of time (as if they did not want to miss any of the actions of the others) just broken by glances to the video channel window. Apparently paradoxically, some of the subjects reported that they had no difficulty in attracting others' attention. The ease of editing and talking simultaneously about objects in the editing surface seemed to provide a reason for this. The editing surface quickly becomes cluttered during long design sessions (especially with larger groups). The same happens with the text medium.

The co-authors also declared they had pursued group-wide discussions, plans about the contents of the documents they were about to produce and plans of who should do what.

We analyse now each of the experiment hypotheses of Sect. 6.4.3.

H.1 Most of the subjects answered that these were quite important; multiple-cursors and WYSIWIS were qualified as indispensable. They felt comfortable gesturing. The subjects did not have serious problems distinguishing who was doing what.

H.2 Most of the subjects answered that this happened. Not having to think about consistency of versions or copies, integration and revisions was reported as a main benefit of the prototype.

H.3 Most of the subjects answered that the brainstorming zone was expressive enough. Also, the resulting editing objects often did not make sense by themselves. They could only be interpreted in the context of the accompanying dialogue or interaction of the participants, i.e. gestures, in addition to which the process of creating and using the editing objects conveys important information not found in the resulting document. This observation is especially apparent with gestures transmitted over the video channel and voice over the audio channel, which do not leave behind any lasting record yet do communicate significant information. It is through the process of seeing how those marks are created and referred to, along with the accompanying verbal explanation, that the group can come to an agreement of what the editing objects mean.

H.4 Most subjects answered that they were acceptable. They appreciated the feature that the annotations and comments could contain several media and used mostly the audio medium. The feature allowing private annotations to be converted to public comment was also mentioned. The subjects reported frustration in accessing them (too many buttons clicked) and commented on the speed with which audio comments were transmitted to the other co-authors (network dependent).

H.5 Most of the subjects answered that the information about other co-authors was possibly not enough, although there were no suggestions for augmenting it. Concerning the usefulness, they reported that in principle it was useful but in practice sparsely used.

H.6 Most of the subjects answered that the multimedia communication channels were very useful. The audio channel was the most used and the co-authors really relied on it for informal and contextual communication. The video channel helped the co-authors not to "feel alone", and its speed was not very important. The text channel was used, although seldom, to express already discussed ideas or facts to be used further on in the editing session. The co-authors reported that audio and video communication recording would be useful.

H.7 Most of the subjects answered that better expertise was available especially if the group was distributed over a wide area. Mainly in the case of the cooperative software production the dependence on the other co-authors was more noticed. Groups connected over a WAN can use physical material that is available to only one of them.

H.8 Most of the subjects answered that they did not feel any particular anxiety to engage in social contacts; the initial (prior to the session beginning) contact tended to be shorter and cooler.

H.9 Most of the subjects answered that uninhibited behaviour occurred more frequently. The co-authors participated more equally than they would do in a face-to-face situation. Due to the multimedia channels, people felt distant and less threatened by the existing ranking. Although the same person tended to dominate in face-to-face situations and in computer-supported editing sessions, this dominance was weaker. No result could be found on the amount of simultaneous speech and the time between speakers.

H.10 Most of the subjects answered that, although the social contacts were fewer, whenever conflicts or uncertain meanings appeared, the multimedia communication channels (audio and video) were mostly used to solve them. More generally, they reported that CoMEdiA helped to solve conflict and disagreement.

H.11 Most of the subjects answered that they did not even think about the physical location of the information. They also did not report about delays due to remote access to the files.

H.12 Most of the subjects answered that they took longer to reach consensus than they thought they would have in a face-to-face situation. This might be because they would have had difficulty in reaching agreement anyway judging by their arguments. They also reported they exchanged fewer remarks. For neither of these aspects was typing or other technology-induced delay a reason.

6.6 Comparison with Existing Systems

Following the same strategy as in Sects. 3.2 and 4.5 as an evaluation mechanism, we now evaluate CoMEdiA and compare it with the systems explained in Sect. 2.4. The goal is to build a table relating technology-level factors with group benefits. We do not present the complete tables (for space reasons) but only the technology-level factors and the total group benefits.

We then compare CoMEdiA with some of the systems of Sect. 2.4.2. We do not compare it with all the systems, because for some of them we do not have all the necessary information about the technology-level factors.

This quantitative comparison gives a fuzzy idea of the potentialities of the several products and prototype systems (see also Fig. 6.4). Nevertheless, it has some pitfalls; for example, when a system provides audio communication, should it be considered multimedia communication or not? Another example are the systems that have annotation capabilities that can vary in expressiveness (several media), power or additional attached functionalities. Also, there are systems that provide "special purpose" features that are not present in the majority of the editors (e.g. messaging and notification facilities).

	CoMEdiA	shrEdit	SASSE	Grove	DistEdit	QuEdit	PREP	XGroupSketch	GroupDraw	GroupGraPhic	AspectS	Slate
1	13	13	13	-	-	13	13	13	13	13	13	13
2	4	-	-	-	-	-	-	4	4	-	4	-
3	10	10	-	10	10	10	10	-	-	-	10	-
4	13	13	13	13	-	13	13	13	13	13	13	13
5	21	21	21	21	21	21	21	21	21	21	21	21
6	18	18	18	18	18	18	18	18	18	18	18	18
7	6	6	6	6	6	6	6	6	6	6	6	6
8	14	-	14	-	-	14	14	-	-	-	-	14
9	7	9	7	7	-	7	7	7	7	7	7	7
10	8	8	8	8	8	8	8	8	8	8	8	8
11	-	5	-	5	-	5	5	-	-	5	-	5
12	-	-	7	7	-	7	7	-	-	7	-	-
13	14	14	-	-	-	-	-	-	-	-	14	14
14	13	-	-	13	-	13	-	-	-	-	-	-
15	-	11	11	11	11	11	11	11	11	11	11	11
16	-	10	10	10	10	-	-	10	10	10	10	10
17	12	12	12	-	12	12	12	12	12	12	12	12
	153	150	140	129	96	158	145	123	123	131	147	152

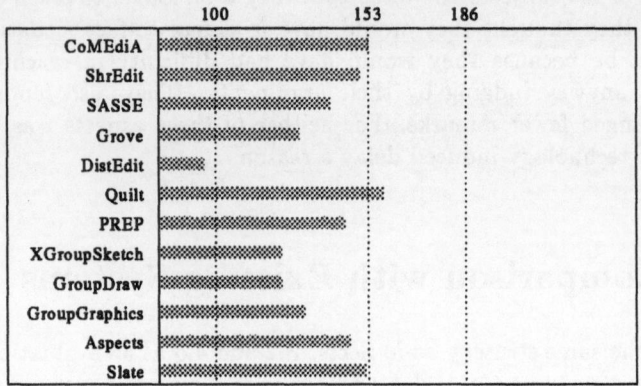

Fig. 6.4: A quantitative comparison of CoMEdiA with other products

Chapter 7

Concluding Remarks

*"Meetings do not take place (exclusively) in
conference rooms."*

7.1 Summing Up

We think that the time for cooperative multimedia editing has come. The
technology now has increased multimedia processing power and networking
bandwidth. Availability and market penetration of these technologies has
reached the critical level and standards are being developed and approaching
their definitive form. On the other hand, theory in the fields of multimedia processing, multimedia communication and cooperation has been around
for several years, and bridges to prototypical practice are now possible. Finally, the market is demanding in this area, and industry is starting to pull
technology, prototypes and concepts together.

In this book, we started by stating that most of the necessary technology
for cooperative multimedia editing is available. This includes, for example, JPEG, MPEG, ADPCM, ODA, audio and video boards for multimedia
processing, and the availability of ISDN routers, PCT/IP, ISDN and Ethernet for multimedia communication. Several categorisations of multimedia
have been given, namely under activity, communication, general and face-
to-face perspectives. The concepts of task, activity, coordination and cooperation are becoming well understood. On the other hand, it has been
possible to clarify a classification of computer-supported cooperative work in
several fields, enabling an identification of the potentials and obstacles for
computer-supported groups. Also, the first prototypes of cooperative multimedia editing have already begun to emerge, demonstrating its feasibility
and usefulness.

Several studies have been performed on groups, cooperative work, collaboration, etc. in recent decades. Mainly, they have been performed by social or organisational psychologists, management scientists, and definitely not by computer scientists. Only with the wide spread of information technology and telecommunications, was the idea of supporting groups using computers born. Reflecting and taking advantage of this development, we have used a widely accepted framework, which describes how groups work and coordinate their actions. This framework can be augmented easily and with modularity to include new aspects of group work. The nature of cooperative multimedia editing implied that not only group processes and dynamics have to be included, but also factors such as technology and time flow. In order to take the best advantages of its potentialities, we augmented it with three extra factors which were not included, namely multimedia technology, computer support and time flow.

The framework used is a descriptive model of group behaviour focusing on the group tasks, having as main concepts: the group input, the group outcomes and the group coordination process that supports the group activity. It is useful in sorting out the relationships among the initial state of a group, the group interaction and the group performance.

The framework does not account for the possibility of computer-supported groups, multimedia technologies and time. Because of these deficiencies we augmented it to include new input factors (computer support and multimedia technology) that influence the group output. We stated that there is a sequential relationship from technology-level input factors to group benefits through group coordination effects. We describe each of the technology-level input factors which roughly correspond to mechanisms or features that induce changes in work habits and techniques (group coordination effects). In the same way, the group coordination effects then influence the group benefits.

Once we had a way of describing group work (more specifically cooperative multimedia editing) and a strategy to evaluate tools, we wanted to build a prototype tool to test the model. We described the conceptualisation of a prototype tool - CoMEdiA - for cooperative multimedia editing. The most important aspects were the multi-user interface, the support for cooperation, the multimedia editing and the multimedia communication.

Multi-user interfaces are conceptually very different from single-user interfaces. The latter realises the interaction between an application and only one user, while the former is concerned with a whole group of people. Such aspects as the amount and complexity of input and output, as well as the model necessary to represent the user(s) make the difference. Other important aspects are the selection of the kind of single-user interface mechanisms, techniques and concepts that are useful for multi-user interfaces. A multi-user interface must depict the overall group activity without being too distracting or disturbing to any of the individual co-authors. In addition, the user requirements come from a whole group and can be incompatible with the individual requirements of each co-author.

Cooperative editing has a number of requirements that are characteristic of multi-user systems. Examples are the ability of the co-authors to work simultaneously on a shared editing surface which helps them to communicate since more work can be done in parallel. In addition, co-authors should have concurrent access to the editing space, the editing functionalities and the document files. Different co-authors should be able to select different tools and different objects, as well as command different operations simultaneously or in any possible temporal order. On the other hand, transitions between activities, such as brainstorming, outlining, editing, reviewing or communicating should be transparent and easy, since they do not always occur in sequence. In addition, viewing, gesturing, editing should be independent of each other in the sense that they should be possible at any time and in any temporal sequence. Each co-author should be able to perform any action independently of the existence of other co-authors in the editing session and of what they are doing.

Although multimedia communication has been presented as a technological wonder for increasing group information and productivity, we note that face-to-face meetings are still the dominant "medium" of communication and face-to-face interactions are still worlds away from computer (multi-)mediated communication. The latter cannot still substitute the former, being limited to a complementary interaction role. Face-to-face meetings are still the most desirable medium despite the difficulties of scheduling and efficiency. Besides, video-conferencing, which is said to best approximate face-to-face meetings, has become a synonym for marketing disaster. Despite the apparent effectiveness of using tele-communication for regular activities, there is something unique about the social contact achieved in a face-to-face meeting. Even in the most successful applications, regular face-to-face contacts have proved indispensable. Also, an increase in communication media does not always imply better communication quality or more use (e.g. no co-author uses the audio and text communication channel simultaneously).

Following the conceptualisation, we described how we realised CoMEdiA. We touched on the aspects of the multi-user interface, the support for cooperation, the multimedia editing and the multimedia communication. Moreover, we described the software architecture and algorithm used, as well as an analysing its performance. In addition, we explained how the prototype tool is described by the models presented before.

As CoMEdiA is basically intended at simulating (replacing) face-to-face editing. We can compare it with both traditional group editing meetings and single-user computer-supported editing processes. CoMEdiA multimedia features can substitute and integrate the use of different single-media applications. Annotations and comments substitute margin jottings. Synchronous communication and WYSIWIS are intended to replace face-to-face communication and version merging. Asynchronous communication is useful if a co-author misses a meeting. The multimedia communication channels were designed to assist the co-authors with the quick exchange of ideas, planning, conceptualisation, coordination and informal side talks. CoMEdiA's selective tele-pointing substitutes the frequent action of calling the attention of whole group. Co-authors' identification and login features provide protection and authorisation features.

A set of issues is posed by the inherent existence of parallelism control problems in cooperative editing. A basic conceptual difference between distributed and cooperative systems is that the former strive to give the user the illusion of being the system's only user, while the latter attempt to make each user's actions visible, and meaning clear, to the others. Groupware presents a unique set of parallelism problems and many of the approaches to handling parallelism in distributed systems - such as explicit locking or transaction processing - are not only inappropriate but can actually hinder tightly coupled teamwork.

In this work, we have limited our implementation to workstations because they were the only feasible hardware solutions with low cost processing units for each member, high communication availability and multimedia processing. Nevertheless, the conceptualisation made is independent of the platform and CoMEdiA has been implemented in such a generic way as to make it as much independent of the platform as possible. An analysis of the effort that would be necessary if other platforms (other workstation vendors, personal computers, NeXT and Apple) had to be considered has been made.

Having achieved the models and the prototype tool, we proceeded with a study of several evaluation methods to find the most suitable to evaluate CoMEdiA. The necessity for evaluation is great, because industry partners must be aware of the group benefits for the users and for itself. It is necessary to enumerate and qualify these. The research in this field can become useful for the public if the functionality of the prototypes is adopted by the software industry and end-users. For this there must be a strong cost/benefit reasoning in the implementation of groupware products. We evaluated CoMEdiA using two different evaluation methods and using the evaluation strategy developed together with the framework. We also made an assessment of the performance of the networks used (Ethernet LAN, Internet WAN and ISDN WAN), the CoMEdiA editing (text, raster images and 2D-graphics), the CoMEdiA audio communication channel and the CoMEdiA video communication channel. On the other hand, we elaborated a questionnaire to get feedback from the co-authors that used the prototype. We made an analysis of the answers and combined them with our own experience and with knowledge acquired from informal talks with co-authors. The results of this evaluation effort were presented as statistics tables, questionnaires answers, a test of twelve experimental hypotheses and a quantitative evaluation.

7.2   Conclusions

The first important result is that the CoMEdiA prototype tool runs success-fully, demonstrating its usability and usefulness, as well as suiting the purpose it was conceived to. General crashes are seldom and the editing sessions and demonstrations run without problems, although once in a while the proto-type crashes (as with almost any research prototype). There are no problems attributable to the heterogeneity of the platforms used. This demonstrates the viability of building applications that can be run in different hardware platforms and configurations. Crashes due to a network failure are very rare which demonstrates that an application can be successfully built to run in different networks (Ethernet, Internet and ISDN).

Co-authors who have been using CoMEdiA have expressed enthusiasm for the prototype tool and for the technology. They articulated that they felt comfortable with it, found it, overall, easy and natural to use and a means of good editing work and communication. The editing media available were said to be sufficiently expressive. CoMEdiA does not impose a barrier be-tween individual and cooperative modes of working. It provides groups with access to individual spaces, allowing them to work privately and facilitating the import of individual knowledge to the group. It does not impose the co-operative mode but rather offers the co-authors freedom to choose their own style. Comparing the system with a face-to-face situation, they considered they had produced an output in less time and with better quality, but opin-ions varied on whether there had been less stress (perhaps due to technology) or more user satisfaction. Apart from the graphical output quality, they re-ported satisfaction with the results obtained. They reported frustration when drawing with the mouse. A stylus would have been an improvement.

Co-authors who had been using CoMEdiA agreed on that CoMEdiA was easy to learn and work with. This can be attributed to the analogy of many of the mechanisms used in CoMEdiA to the typical paper-and-pen situation, to the problem-oriented approach (instead of a task-oriented one) and to the simple syntax.

As with any other innovation, and most innovations fail on the market, cooperative multimedia editing has to burst some barriers in order to progress from research prototypes to products. We think that there are three cate-gories of reasons that could lead to failure of the introduction of cooperative multimedia editing products to industry. Technical misalignments, which occur when the product does not fit with the processes into which it is intro-duced, structure misalignments, which result from a lack of fit between the product and the technical or organisational infrastructure, and value mis-alignments, which occur when the product fails to meet the performance criteria of the end-users or sponsors. Unfortunately, there are still very few true success stories of group software products on the market. The differ-ent approaches described in this work provide a clue to the current range of experience but also show that little end-user experience is available.

The fact that multimedia communication cannot fully substitute face-to-face meetings has led us to examine ways of approximating the functionality of both. Audio and video channels might provide the basis for the informal communication present in face-to-face meetings when supporting remote meetings. We think these multimedia channels can be useful for increasing the overall amount of information transmitted, increasing participation, spontaneity and frequency of communication, supporting social relationships and consensus development and, finally, supporting the most complex and equivocal communication. In other words, non-multimedia communication reduces communication efficiency, especially concerning the above "less technical" aspects, even though multimedia and non-multimedia communication are roughly equivalent for pure information transfer tasks.

Other findings from our work concerning multimedia communication are that co-authors using it exchange fewer remarks, take longer to reach consensus, make more task-oriented remarks or explicit decision proposals, participate more equally, exhibit uninhibited behaviour, do not speak simultaneously as long or as often and can initiate communication more easily.

Also, during our experiments, we noticed important differences between video and face-to-face contacts. Unlike eyes, cameras have a fixed field of view and usually cannot be controlled by the viewer. Failure to make eye contact is problematic because of the separation of camera and display. The principle of reciprocity does not always hold and there is no negotiated mutual distance between speakers, nor do they have any sense of how their voices are perceived by listeners. There is relative impotence of gestures and gaze in securing other's attention and in avoiding the feeling of being "distant" from others. It is also difficult to be aware of who, if anyone, is visually attending to oneself, to listen selectively to different, parallel conversations and to make asides to other persons.

Although gestures and motions transmitted over a video channel do not leave behind any persistent record in the drawing space, we suggest that they can be used to store information. Our experience during this work revealed that co-authors did not experience any problems in remembering gestures later in the editing session or even in later sessions. One aid to remembering is for other co-authors to imitate a gesture. Gestures and movements transmitted via a video channel are particularly well-suited to demonstrate a sequence of actions, such as a person interacting with a machine.

We also concluded that voice communication is most important for the co-authors' communication. These reported that they prefer improvement of the audio channel over addition a video channel or improvement to it. In contrast, they admitted that tasks involving object-related discussions can hardly be done with audio channels only. Additionally, co-authors reported that text channels also have positive aspects, namely the communication is non-ephemeral.

Once people have access to computer-mediated communication, their status, power, and prestige are communicated neither contextually (e.g. the way secretaries, meeting rooms and clothes communicate) nor dynamically (e.g. the nature of gaze). Communication technology that reduces the importance of status and dominance could increase the likelihood that opinions in groups are sampled more widely. Also, if charismatic and high-status people have less influence, then group members may participate more equally. If people who are high in status usually talk most and dominate meetings, then computer-mediated communication that de-emphasises the impact of status also might increase people's consideration of minority views. If minority opinions, wide opinion sampling and more equal participation can enhance performance, then computer-mediated communication can help groups to be more effective.

Our results concerning the adequacy of each of the networks we tried showed that within an Ethernet LAN there are absolutely no performance or responsiveness problems. The transmission times are rather constant, and the transmission rate grows with the size of the messages (apparently the network tries to respond to more network load with more bandwidth). With an Internet WAN, the response delays are highly dependent on the network load (as expected) and the responsiveness is low. This network should just be used in exceptional cases when no other network is available. As a circuit-switched network, ISDN WAN has constant transmission rates. Nevertheless, those observed are not as advertised by the vendors. This may be because we used a router and a terminal adapter to bridge from the LAN to the ISDN. This introduces overhead from the conversion and routing of the packets, and from the use of a piece of the LAN (between the machines and the routers). This would have been avoided if we had re-programmed the communication layer of CoMEdiA to use ISDN directly.

A pitfall of today's multimedia integrated products is that users may easily think that the specific functionalities they find in these systems are not so powerful as the ones they would be using in different stand-alone specialised systems. This represents a inevitable trade-off between the values of integration and the power within specific solutions. Moreover, integrated systems are also likely to be expensive to produce and are probably not compatible with the mainstream software market.

We assessed that the text and the raster images media are the most used. 2D-graphics are used when the task requires more exact output or more graphical composition work. The audio medium is very much used for comments and annotations. The video is a very special-purpose medium, only used for special tasks, e.g. the one in the second experimental case application (cooperative technical data production).

Documents that are worked out in cooperative editing sessions are group compositions that emerge from the contributions of individuals. The mechanism for generating information can consist of unconnected editing (a co-author enters information while paying little attention to what is already there or what is being discussed), meditative editing (a co-author comments on, appends to, or modifies what has already been entered), agreement editing (as the result of discussion within the group new editing or modifications are done to the document), refinement editing (the group assigns particular members to refine or reorganise particular parts of the document), and scribe editing (a co-author para-phrases what is being discussed via the multimedia communication channels).

An important aspect in cooperative editing is the parallel access to information. Groupware systems need parallelism control to resolve conflicts between simultaneous operations. We developed an algorithm and architecture that support cooperative tasks, and whose main roles are to maintain a global coherence state of the cooperative system and to control the information flow amongst the co-authors. The algorithm and architecture employed have to serialise co-authors' requests, guarantee mutual exclusion on the access, ensure global consistency of the documents, maintain responsiveness at a high level, have the capacity to support wide-area distribution, support data replication and be robust to failures.

The most important mechanisms used to build multi-user interfaces are multiple-cursors, tele-pointing, gesturing and WYSIWIS. Also, we noticed that of all the WYSIWIS variants, Relaxed-WYSIWIS is the best for general purpose, informal group activities, although Strict-WYSIWIS should also be available. During editing, co-authors frequently gesture over the editing surface to represent ideas, to signal turn-taking, to focus the attention of the group, to reference objects, etc. Multi-cursors, tele-pointing and WYSIWIS are mostly used for this. We believe that these mechanisms can also improve communication quality and participant awareness.

Intuitively, to generate ideas the best way is to assemble a group of people and brainstorm. However, research on non-computer-supported brainstorming reveals that a set of individuals can get more and better ideas by working by themselves and pooling their ideas than by working as an interacting group. The reasons for this are known to be evaluation fear, free riding, linear air time, production blocking and cognitive inertia. Production blocking (due to limited air time, individuals have to hold on to ideas until they get a chance to contribute, and as a result they might forget or decide not to add them) is the dominant reason for the reduced productivity. With the kind of computer support for brainstorming that we provide, production blocking and air time are no longer negative factors, because people can contribute as much time as they want and do not have to do it synchronously or in a particular temporal order. Cognitive inertia is also avoided because different subgroups or even individuals can follow several ideas simultaneously and even inter-change between them. In contrast, evaluation fear and free riding are not eliminated.

Of the several ways of defining a proper behaviour of the co-authors, namely defined only by the group members, by the software or inbetween, we defend the second as the most feasible. The first is the most flexible but also the most complex for the co-authors to understand and to use properly. Moreover, it is very costly to implement in a software product. The second reduces coordination problems by specifying responsibilities, permissible actions, restrictions, and patterns of interaction for the co-authors.

Co-authors who had been using CoMEdiA also declared they had pursued group-wide discussions, plans about the contents of the documents they were about to produce and plans of who should do what. They also said their plans did change a little during the editing itself. In addition, they added that consistency of the overall work and constant validation were eased. Not having to think about consistency of versions or copies, integration and revisions was reported as a main benefit of the prototype tool.

We can also conclude that mechanisms for annotation (private) and commenting (public) are useful. Indeed, co-authors appreciate features such as annotations and comments which can contain several media (especially the audio medium). Also important is the feature to turn a private annotation into a public comment.

We noticed that non-face-to-face editing groups can have access to better available expertise and possibly richer information and technological environments. This is especially true if the group is distributed over a wide area. For example, in the first experimental case application (cooperative software engineering) the dependence on other co-authors was more noticed. Groups connected over a WAN can use physical material that is available to only one of them (e.g. user manuals, include file, libraries).

8   References

[Applegate 91] Applegate L., "Technology support for cooperative work: A framework for studying introduction and assimilation in organisations", Journal of Organisational Computing, 1, p.11-39.

[Baecker et al. 92] Baecker R., Nastos D., Posner I., Mawby K., "The user-centred iterative design of collaborative writing software", in Proc. Workshop for real-time group drawing and writing tools, Toronto, Nov.

[Bair 89] Bair J., "Supporting cooperative work with computers: Addressing meeting mania", in Proc. COMPCON'89, 34 IEEE Computer Society International Conference, San Francisco, CA.

[Beck et al. 93] Beck E., "Informed opportunism as strategy: Supporting coordination in distributed collaborative writing", in Proc. ECSCW'93, Milan, Sept.

[Biel 91] Biel V., "Groupware groups up", MacUser, June.

[Bly et al. 90] Bly S., Minneman S., "Commune: A shared drawing surfaces", in Proc. COIS'90, Cambridge, ACM Press, Baltimore, MD, p.184-192.

[Bodker et al. 88] Bodker S., Ehn P., Knudsen J., Kyng M., Madsen K., "Computer support for cooperative design", in Proc. CSCW'88, Portland, ACM Press, Baltimore, MD.

[Brinck et al. 92] Brinck T., Gomez L., "A collaborative medium for the support of conversational props", in Proc. CSCW'92, Toronto, ACM Press, p.171-178.

[Brothers et al. 90] Brothers L., Sembugamoorthy, M., "ICICLE: Groupware for code inspection", in Proc. CSCW'90, Los Angeles, CA.

[Co-Tech WG3 93] Andriessen E., Hjerppe R., Jungert E., Kehrer T., Lubich H., Peiró J., Rugelj J., Santos A., van der Velden J., Wilbur S., "Multimedia-supported cooperation: concepts, applications and technical support requirements", in Report of Co-Tech Working Group 3, Wilbur S., Lubich H., Santos A. (ed.), January.

[Egido 89] Egido C., "Tele-conferencing as a technology to support cooperative work: Its possibilities and limitations", in Intellectual teamwork: Social and technological foundations of cooperative work, Galegher J., Kraut R., Egido C. (ed.), Lawrence Erlbaum Associates, p.351-372.

[Ellis et al. 91] Ellis C., Gibbs S., Rein G., "Groupware: Some issues and experiences", Communications of the ACM, Vol. 34, No. 1, Jan.

[Encarnação 88] Encarnação J., W. Strasser "Computer Graphics", München, Oldenburg Verlag.

[Encarnação 91] Encarnação J., Astheimer P., Felger W., Frühauf M., Göbel M., Karlsson K., "Graphics Modeling as a basic tool for scientific visualization", in Modeling in Computer Graphics, Kunii T. (ed.), Tokyo, Springer-Verlag, p.293-315.

[Encarnação 94] Encarnação J., Foley J., "Multimedia, System architectures and applications", Proceedings of Dugstuhl Workshop 9245, Berlin, Springer-Verlag.

[Encarnação 94] Encarnação J., Santos A., "Frontiers of Computer Technology", Proceedings of IEEE TENCON'94, Singapore, IEEE.

[Engelbart 88] Engelbart D., "Toward high-performance knowledge workers", in Greif I., (ed.), Computer-Supported Cooperative Work: A Book of Readings, Morgan Kaufman, San Mateo, CA, p.108-126.

[Fish et al. 88] Fish R., Kraut R., Leland M., Cohen M., "Quilt: A collaborative tool for cooperative writing", in Proc. COIS'88, Conference on office information systems.

[Fish et al. 92] Fish R., Kraut R., Root R., "Evaluating video as a technology for informal communication", in Proc. CHI'92, p.37-47.

[Galegher et at. 90a] Galegher J., Kraut R., "Technology for intellectual teamwork: Perspectives on research and design", in Intellectual teamwork: Social and technological foundations of cooperative work, Galegher J., Kraut R., Egido C. (ed.), Lawrence Erlbaum Associates, p.1-20.

[Greenberg 91a] Greenberg S., "Computer-supported cooperative work and groupware", Academic Press.

[Greenberg et al. 92] Greenberg S., Roseman M., Webster D., "Human and Technical Factors of Distributed Group Drawing Tools", in Interacting with Computers, special issue on CSCW, Dec.

[Greif 88] Greif I., Computer-supported cooperative work: A book of readings, Morgan Kaufmann, San Mateo, CA.

[Hackman 83] Hackman J., "The design of work teams", In Handbook of organisational behaviour", Lorsch J. (ed.), Prentice-Hall, Englewood Cliffs, NJ

[Hackman et al. 86] Hackman J., Walton R., "Leading groups in organisations", In Designing effective work teams, Goodman P. (ed.), Jossey-Bass, New York.

[Hornung et al. 91a] Hornung C., Santos A., "CoMEdiA: A cooperative hypermedia editing architecture: The problem of the cooperative access", in Multimedia: systems, interaction, and applications, Kjelldahl L. (ed.), Berlin, Springer-Verlag.

[Hornung et al. 91b] Hornung C., Santos A., "A proposal for a reference model for cooperative hypermedia systems", in Multimedia: systems, interaction, and applications, Kjelldahl L. (ed.), Berlin, Springer-Verlag.

[Hornung et al. 93a] Hornung C., Jäger M., Santos A., Tritsch B., "Cooperative Hyper-Media - An Enabling Paradigm for Cooperative Work", The Visual Computer, special edition on Techniques and applications of computer graphics in the context of telecommunications, Vol. 9, 6, May.

[Hornung et al. 93b] Hornung C., Santos A., "Cooperative user interfaces and networks for collaboration", Tutorial notes, EUROGRAPHICS'93 Conference, Barcelona, Sept.

[Hymowitz 88] Hymowitz C., "A survival guide to the office meeting", Wall Street Journal, June 21.

[Ishii et al. 91] Ishii H., Miyake N., "Towards a open shared workspace: Computer and video fusion approach of TeamWorkStation", in Communication of the ACM, Vol. 34, No.12, Dec., p.37-50.

[Jäger 92] Jäger M., "MISTER COOL: Das multi-mediale diensteintegrierende ISDN Endgerät", GRIS 92-4, Research report, Technical University Darmstadt.

[Johansen 88] Johansen R., "Groupware: computer support for business teams", The Free Press, New York.

[Johansen 89] Johansen R., "User approaches to computer-support teams", in Technological support for work group collaboration, Olson M. (ed.), Lawrence Erlbaum
Associates, Hillsdale, NJ, p.1-32.

[Kerr et al. 92] Kerr E., Hiltz S., "Computer-mediated communication systems", Academic Press, New York.

[Knister et al. 90] Knister M., Prakash A., "DistEdit: A distributed toolkit for supporting
multiple group editors", in Proc. CSCW'90, Los Angeles, CA.

[Kraemer et al. 88] Kraemer K., King J., "Computer-based systems for cooperative work",
Computing Surveys, 20, June, p.115-146.

[Kraut et al. 88] Kraut R., Egido C., "Patterns of contact and communication in scientific
communication", in Proc. CSCW'88, Portland, ACM Press, Baltimore, MD.

[Kraut et al. 92] Kraut R., Fish R., "Audio/video networks for collaboration", Tutorial
notes, CSCW '92, Toronto, ACM Press.

[Lamport 78] Lamport L., "Time, clocks, and the ordering of events in a distributed system", Communications of the ACM, July.

[Marcos 92] Marcos A., "Cooperative Editing of Static Images and 2D-Graphics in Co-
MEdiA", in report FIGD - 92i014.

[McGrath 84] McGrath J., "Groups: Interaction and performance", Prentice-Hall, Englewood Cliffs, NJ

[McGuffin 92] McGuffin L., Olson G., "ShrEdit: A shared electronic workspace", Cognitive science and machine intelligence laboratory, University of Michigan, Technical
report #45.

[Neuwirth et al. 90] Neuwirth C., Kaufer D., Chandhok R., Morris J., "Issues in the design
of computer support for co-authoring and commenting", in Proc. CSCW'90, Los
Angeles, CA.

[Newman-Wolfe et al. 92] Newman-Wolfe R., Webb M., Montes M., "Implicit locking
in the Ensemble concurrent object-oriented graphics editor", in Proc. CSCW'92,
Toronto, ACM Press, p.265-272.

[Nunamaker et al. 91] Nunamaker J., Dennis A., Valacich J., Vogel D., George F., "Electronic meeting systems to support group work", Communications of the ACM, 34,
7, July, p.40-61.

[Olson et al. 90] Olson J., Olson G., Mack L., Wellner P., "Concurrent editing: The
group's interface", in Proc. IFIP'90, Elsevier (North-Holland).

[Pendergast 92] Pendergast M., "GroupGraphics: Prototype and product", in Proc. Workshop for real-time group drawing and writing tools, Toronto, Nov.

[Ricart et al. 81] Ricart G., Agrawala A., "An optimal algorithm for mutual exclusion in
computer networks", Communications of the ACM, Jan.

[Santos 90] Santos A., "State-of-the-Art report on multimedia", Internal report, FAGD-
90i034, Darmstadt, Dec.

[Santos 91] Santos A., "Some issues on cooperative multimedia editing", Quarto Encontro
Portugues de Computação Gráfica, pp.135-154, Lisbon, Nov.

[Santos 92a] Santos A., "A Cooperative architecture for hypermedia editing - CoMEdiA", Computer Graphics Forum, Vol. II, 5, Dec., p.309-322.

[Santos 93a] Santos A., "Cooperative hypermedia editing with CoMEdiA", Journal of Computer Science and Technology, Vol.8, No. 2.

[Santos 93b] Santos A., "Using a cooperative hypermedia editing tool to enhance group communication and productivity", The Visual Computer, Vol. 10, 1.

[Santos 93c] Santos A., Marcos A., "CoMEdiA: Uma ferramenta para a edição cooperativa de informação multimedia", Quinto Encontro Portugues de Computação Gráfica, Aveiro, Feb.

[Santos 93d] Santos A., "CoMEdiA: Conceptualisation and realisation of a cooperative hypermedia editing architecture", Computers & Graphics Magazine, Vol. 17, 3, May/June.

[Santos 93e] Santos A., Tritsch B., "Using multimedia to support cooperative editing", in Proc. EUROGRAPHICS'93 Conference, Barcelona, Sept.

[Santos 93f] Santos A., Marcos A., "An algorithm and architecture to support cooperative multimedia editing", in Proc. Fourth IEEE Workshop on Future Trends of Distributed Computing Systems, Sept., Lisbon.

[Santos 94a] Santos A., "Evaluating multimedia availability for groupware", in Proc. IEEE International Conference on Multimedia Computing Systems, Boston, May.

[Santos 94b] Santos A., Tritsch B., "Cooperative multimedia editing tool for enhanced group communication", in Computer communications, Vol. 17, 4, April, Butterworth-Heinemann

[Santos 94c] Santos A., Theresa M.R., Brett, G., Brutzman D., Cox, D., "Exploiting networks for visualization and collaboration: No network roadblocks", in Computer graphics proceedings, SIGGRAPH'94, Orlando, p.481, Addison Wesley.

[Stefik 86] Stefik M., "WYSIWIS revised: Early experiences with multi-user interfaces", in Proc. CSCW'86, Austin, Texas, ACM Press, Baltimore, MD., p.276-290.

[Stefik et al. 87] Stefik M., Foster G., Bobrow D., Kahn K., Lanning S., Suchman L., "Beyond the chalkboard: Using computers to support collaboration and problem solving in meetings", Communications of the ACM, 30(1), p.32-47.

[Tritsch et al. 92] Tritsch B., Hornung C., "Cooperative multimedia on heterogeneous platforms or how to apply tele-media", in Proc. Dagstuhl workshop on multimedia system architectures and applications, Nov.

[Wilson 92] Wilson B., "Wscrawl 2.0: A shared whiteboard based on X Windows", in Proc. Workshop for real-time group drawing and writing tools, Toronto, Nov.

Springer-Verlag
and the Environment

We at Springer-Verlag firmly believe that an international science publisher has a special obligation to the environment, and our corporate policies consistently reflect this conviction.

We also expect our business partners – paper mills, printers, packaging manufacturers, etc. – to commit themselves to using environmentally friendly materials and production processes.

The paper in this book is made from low- or no-chlorine pulp and is acid free, in conformance with international standards for paper permanency.